song "Angels among us by Alabama

TWO HEARTS, ONE HOPE

A True Story of Enduring Faith
in the Messiness of Life

KARLIE GREEN

TWO HEARTS, ONE HOPE

A True Story of Enduring Faith in the Messiness of Life

Published by The Long Road Publishing.

ISBN: 978-0-578-67981-5. First edition.

To Mom—thank you for teaching me about a God who loves, forgives, and saves.

To Kylie—this book was a dream of ours six years ago. Today, this is all for you. Thank you for taking care of me for thirty-five years and now still from Heaven. I love you.

Contents

This book is a memoir. It reflects the author's present recollections of experiences over time. Some names and characteristics have been changed, some events have been abridged, and some dialogue has been supplemented. Names, characters, places, and incidents are based on the author's memories, where others may have conflicting memories. The intent of this work is to encourage the reader to move forward in their life in the face of adversity through faith in God and walking in His love.

CHAPTER ONE

Get Here Now

TEN HOURS. THAT'S HOW LONG the drive is from Amarillo to Houston. In our family, that journey means either a routine health checkup— or something has gone terribly wrong. On April 29th, 2009, something had definitely gone terribly wrong.

The telltale swelling had started a couple of weeks back, on our trip to Hawaii. *Hawaii, y'all!* How could anything bad happen on those beautiful islands? But I'd only been back from the trip for one day before I was kicking myself for taking the flight. After all, the doctors had told me, *We don't advise air travel so soon. Your chances of another blood clot will greatly increase.*

You see, my heart has always beat with only three chambers—one less than most, a story I'll share more of later. It's a resilient organ but doesn't handle complications well. Yes, the doctors were adamant, but as a 25-year old who had lived her whole life with medical warnings, I was ready to live a little. I mean, *Hawaii!* The thought of missing out on once-in-a-lifetime adventures seemed worth pushing the limits.

Not long after I arrived in the islands, I felt a hot tingling around my ankle. *Maybe it's nothing,* I thought. When I saw the swelling, I figured it was from a bad sunburn. I remembered falling asleep on the beach while my girlfriends went cliff-jumping into the Pacific. My body had been too exhausted to climb the rocks. Maybe I should have been concerned then at how tired I had become—but there's nothing like a warm salt breeze to make you forget, well, almost anything.

The coughing started when Dad picked me up from the airport. It began with a tightness, then a catch in my throat, like something needed to dislodge. Annoyance changed to suspicion then shifted to escalating fear. *It felt too familiar.* By the time we pulled into the driveway, I was fighting to inhale. Were my lungs going to end me right here and now? Coming through the doorway, I leaned onto the wood for support and motioned to Dad, unable to speak.

"Karlie? Karlie. Can you breathe?" I stared over his right shoulder and tried to swallow back the lumps in my airway. "Karlie!" He snapped me back.

"Dad," I managed to sputter, "I don't think this is good."

"MmmMmm." He shook his head. Something was dangerously off. I could feel it. We both could. Then he grabbed the keys to my black Mustang. "Karlie, grab some clothes and get in the car."

OH, IT JUST GOT REAL!

My suitcases were still full of swimsuits, beachwear, and some sandy flip-flops. Two days ago I was halfway across the world. Two days ago I could breathe. Amazing how life could change so quickly. I couldn't help but wonder what could happen in another two days.

Throwing together an overnight bag, I walked to the back door and waited as Dad checked the gas in the car. *This is fine. It's nothing. We're overreacting. Right? Please, Lord, let us be overreacting.*

I wondered what my identical twin sister, Kylie, would do if she were there. Throughout our lives, when disaster strikes, she's always been the first person by my side. Some people look to parents, a spouse, or a self-help guru in moments of pressure. From the very beginning, my go-to supporter has always been my twin sister.

But the morning of April 29th, 2009, as we headed to Houston from Amarillo, Kylie wasn't there.

As we drove, Dad drummed his fingers on the steering wheel between my retching coughs. He looked over every time I had a really violent spasm. There was just enough nervousness in his eyes to remind me, *We've been here before. This isn't good.* But there's only so much a dad can do for a daughter who keeps nearly dying. So he did all he could do—he drove faster.

My ankles were now three times their normal size. Granted, at 4'11" I never had especially thick ankles to begin with. My friends still joke with me about whether I shop in the children's section. Being small never fazed me growing up. It just was what it was—just like all the medical tests, surgeries, and shots I endured as a consequence of my heart condition.

Small stature and fragile energy were the cards I had been dealt. Folding wasn't an option, so I just kept playing. Maybe it's my Texas roots, my mom's prayers, or Kylie's unwavering support, but it takes a lot to rattle me. Still, in that car, there was no getting comfortable. My body wouldn't settle; neither would my racing mind. It's difficult when you're coughing up phlegm every few seconds. I went through a full box of tissues. *Are we there yet? Nine hours to go. Eight. Seven. Six....*

My ragged breathing in the car took me back five weeks to another trip to the emergency room. I could see the memory reflected in Dad's unsettled glances. It was my birthday (our birthday, Kylie's and mine.) The ambulance came to our house that night through the snow. I remembered them wanting to put an IV in my neck because they couldn't get one in my arms. Between coughs, I had convinced them I didn't want that, so they chose a vein in my foot along the side of my pinky toe, such a strange place to have an IV. I've never forgotten it. The next day, doctors diagnosed me. A single blood clot, an accidental clumping of platelets, started in my leg, traveled to my lungs, and nearly stopped my breathing. I stayed in the hospital for seven days while they finished stabilizing me, analyzing me, and every other -izing of me they could imagine. The whole time I just wanted to hear two things: *You're going to be okay, and you can go to Hawaii.* It seems like a funny thing to be so set on now, looking back. But in all honesty, understanding the delicate balance of life only made me *more* set on experiencing as much as possible. If I had to choose between a long life of fear or a shorter one full of love and memories—living had to win out over fear.

ONLY 48 HOURS

My dad and I stopped right outside Houston to sleep before my morning appointment. Because of that "birthday clot," Amarillo doctors had wanted me to follow up with a respected pediatric cardiologist in Houston. Pediatricians are most experienced with congenital, or "from birth," heart defects. That would be me. So by the grace of God, we already had an appointment set up.

Do you remember traveling as a kid and being so excited to explore the new hotel room—finding all the cabinets and hiding places and jumping on the beds? As a small kid, I was really good at finding hiding spots. Kylie would help me explore. Motels aren't the same at 25 with your father holding your arm so you don't collapse in the parking lot. He knew my body was giving out. Only later did Dad share that he didn't think I would even make it through the night.

I'm not a stranger to hospitals. My first heart surgery had happened at five months old. I went into Houston's Texas Children's Hospital the next morning with my dad for my scheduled stress test, echocardiogram (Echo) and other "normal" procedures for me. In the moment, that sense of normalcy gave me a foundation to stand on.

After the Echo, Dad and I started to calm down. Everything seemed more normal. A nurse escorted me to a room with a treadmill on it and motioned for me to climb on. These treadmills are for testing the heart under different levels of physical stress. It's like having a strange gym trainer.

But before we could really get started, the doorknob rattled. Another nurse burst into the room and commanded, "Sit down, don't move."

"Is something wrong?" It took everything to keep a steady voice as I sat down.

"We found another clot. It's in your heart."

The blood still running through my veins went clammy cold. I swallowed back a painful lump in my throat and managed to ask, "How—how big is it?"

"About the size of a grapefruit."

Holy—?! How big is a grapefruit again? Is that bigger than a baseball? How does that even fit inside little old me?

"Okay," my mind was whirring. "Without surgery, how long do I have?"

"You would have... about 48 hours."

The next few seconds are forever seared into my memory. I picked up my red Blackberry sitting to the right of me on the patient table. I typed four letters into the contact search: *Yoda*. I texted just three words: "Get here now."

I woke up the next day to the very face I needed to see. My Yoda, my sister, Kylie. Kylie had taken the redeye flight overnight. My nurse let her lay down next to me in the hospital bed, tubes and wires sticking out in all directions. We spent the whole day together while I stayed hooked up to all sorts of machines.

The pumping and whirring created a haunting but strangely comforting white noise, interrupted by mechanical beeps. My sister's 5'11" frame filled up the whole length of the bed. I'm sure next to her I looked pretty frail. But even in the middle of such a traumatic scene, her strong and steady presence cut through my exhaustion.

The sass in her laugh. Gentleness of her words. The loving pressure of her fingers on my hand. It was like something missing had clicked back into place—whatever happened next, we would at least do it together.

The next morning, May 2, 2009, I went in for my 4th open-heart surgery. It was nearly a 10-hour procedure, as long as the tortuous drive from Amarillo. My family was in for more shock, because after surgeons found the grapefruit-sized clot in my heart, they had to scrape my entire left lung. It was fully clotted all the way down to my liver. To this day, I'll never know how I survived long enough to make it to surgery, except that a loving God had His hand on me.

Four days later, I woke up with a heart mechanically set on 80-beats-per-minute. I would always need a pacemaker from that point on to keep my heart beating. But that didn't bother me too much. If Kylie kept me going on the outside, this little mechanical device would keep me going on the inside.

Well, at least that was the plan. The day before my scheduled discharge, sitting on the little hospital room couch with my Dad, I felt a sudden rush of heat. But as I stood to ask him to turn up the air conditioning, my heart went into V-tach (ventricular tachycardia).

I must have collapsed on the floor, because the next thing I remember is my dad slapping the crap out of my face to bring me back. My glasses broke. My nose was cracked and bleeding from falling on the tile floor. My pacemaker recorded a pounding 304 beats per minute—an literally explosive rate.

Friends, I don't know about you, but my life has rarely gone as planned. Bodies fail. People fail. Some days you're basking on a beach in Hawaii. Some days you're hacking out a lung, ten hours away from life-saving surgery. But one thing I have found to be true: it's been the most painful moments of my life—physically and emotionally—that have empowered me to appreciate the true miracles of life, love, and faith with the people who matter most to me.

And the first person on that list is my sister Kylie.

CHAPTER TWO

Red Wagons and Answered Prayer

MARSHA GREEN AND HER HUSBAND Steve were on the way to Central Plains Regional Hospital in Plainview (now called Covenant). Marsha almost couldn't believe it was finally happening. She hugged a diaper bag close to her chest as the car thudded over a bump in the road. Texas scrub-brush whizzed past in the window, broken only by the occasional electric post or speed limit sign.

There had already been months leading up to this day, but could she take just one more minute to get used to it? Each second ticked closer to a lifelong prayer fulfilled. Soon she'd be rocking tiny cries to sleep. Holding messy hands. Teaching, nurturing, disciplining and loving, oh so much loving!

For her entire young life, parenthood had been her greatest dream. But then the first diagnosis came, and her friends said in well-meaning tones, "I guess there's another plan." But that didn't help the hurt inside.

Cancer is always difficult, but there is a unique place of grief, shock, and disbelief saved for young people facing the diagnosis. Marsha had needed the doctor to repeat themselves so she could be sure. Non-Hodgkin's Lymphoma. It was operable, but she needed to fight with everything in her to survive.

Chemo, radiation, it was going to be rough.

In fact, it would be so rough that her doctors couldn't promise that her fertility would survive. Her sister and mother had taken turns driving her back and forth to Plainview for radiation and chemotherapy. She remembered being violently sick all the way home after each session. Somehow, she just knew she had to go through it to survive.

Later that same year, Marsha met Steve Green, fell in love, and married. He knew her chances of motherhood were not great. Because of all the chemo, Marsha's body formed a literal wall around her heart. After open-heart surgery, she was left so weak she developed lupus. The shattering of her body and her dreams took years to overcome, even into recovery, remission, and a new, married life.

Marsha had walked countless grocery store aisles watching mothers toting their toddlers. The cries of babies in public perked her attention. She cried out to God in pain, but also in faith, like Hannah in the Bible:

She was deeply distressed and prayed to the Lord and wept bitterly. And she vowed a vow and said, "O Lord of hosts, if you will indeed look on the affliction of your servant and remember me and not forget your servant, but will give to your servant a son, then I will give him to the Lord all the days of his life, and no razor shall touch his head." (I Samual 1:10)

Why did God put such a strong desire for motherhood into her heart if He wasn't going to give her children? Where had those years planning her future family gone?

Sometime after a heart-wrenching miscarriage, Marsha's doctor told her that she needed a hysterectomy. But still, she and her husband kept praying. Like Hannah in the temple, they brought their requests to God. And every day, it seemed, He responded, *I love you, but not yet. I love you, but not yet. I love you, but not yet.* Every day for years it was the same prayer. And every day, Marsha continued to watch the toddlers and listen to the babies and pray.

Her answer arrived with a cousin's visit one afternoon. "Marsha, my friend's daughter has found herself in a… *situation.*" Unwed motherhood wasn't uncommon in those rural areas, but still, people talked about it carefully.

"Does she need help?" Marsha had asked. "Diapers? Food?"

"She wants to adopt, well, put him up for adoption."

After so much heartbreak, Marsha couldn't believe her ears. Could this finally be the answer to her prayers?

"Yes. Yes! We want that sweet baby boy!" They told everyone about their soon-to-be son.

On March 27, 1984, a sixteen-year-old girl went into labor. She hadn't planned on a family so soon. She could barely take care of herself. She was single, terrified and dying for the comfort of a fix, but for the last nine months had carried life inside of her—a life she hoped might have a better chance. Because for all of the pain, fear, and addiction, something had stirred her heart.

Something had whispered to her heart, *Trust me.*

Marsha and Steve arrived at the hospital and dashed through to the maternity ward. They found the large, glass window and began scanning the rows of squish-faced babies. The nurse saw their excited faces, smiled, and pointed at one particular bassinet.

Marsha squealed with excitement and clutched Steve's hand. Wrapped in little knit blankets were… two babies! Not one boy, but two identical little girls. (I was exactly one minute older, a fact I never let Kylie forget.) My new Mom named me Karlie Le Shea Green and our new Dad named my sister Kylie Re Nee' Green.

My mother's prayers were answered. My sister and I had found our new home. And the adventure of our two hearts was just beginning.

LITTLE GIRL BLUE

I used to wonder why anyone enjoyed running—maybe you're with me on that. To see my friends finish marathons, even a "light" 5K, with a look of triumph, impresses me. But if I'm honest, I'm also a little jealous.

For me, the thought of physical exertion triggers memories of gasping in panic with a desperate tightness in my chest, like being held underwater just a second too long. To this day, I catch myself asking friends, "Are you ok?" as they cross that finish line.

They always are, but I have to ask, because if it were me—I wouldn't be.

Tricuspid Atresia affects five in 100,000 American births. I guess I've always been lucky. Now, to make a fancy medical term a little more practical, here's a quick biology lesson. (There won't be a quiz, promise! :)

Your heart is the most important muscle in your body. It pumps 24/7, 365 days a year, and most people never have to think twice about it working. What an amazing creation!

Like most people, your heart probably formed with four distinct chambers: a left atrium and ventricle and a right atrium and ventricle. The left chambers receive blue, oxygen-poor blood and send it to your lungs for a nice breath. The right chambers take that oxygen-rich blood and pump it to the rest of your body.

To keep that all-important blood flowing in the right direction, each chamber has one entrance and one exit— these are the valves. Each one has a name. The one that caused me the most trouble is the *tricuspid* valve. See, while every other part of my heart grew properly, that one never arrived. It stood me up. Without a valve to let the blood in, my right lower heart chamber (ventricle) didn't develop. It's just a flappy piece of skin.

So instead of a four-chambered heart, I only have three.

Well, what does that mean? For me, this heart problem equals an oxygen problem. My missing chamber was in charge of sending oxygen-poor blood to the lungs. Without the right chamber, some of that blood gets lost along the way. It misses out on that life-giving oxygen— but gets pumped to the body anyway. Whenever I hear the phrase "blue-blood" I chuckle inside.

Tell me about it.

My cells are always searching for air. People with this condition tire easily, are often short of breath—sometimes that blue blood even gives us blue skin! Babies with T/A are actually called "blue babies."

My sister was born with congenital heart problems too: VSD (Ventricular Septal Defect). A VSD is a hole in the heart's septum. This wall separates the heart's lower chambers and lets blood cross from the left to the right side of the heart. Because of VSD, Kylie's oxygen-rich blood got pumped *back* to the lungs instead of out to the body, which means more work for the heart. Thankfully, many VSD and other small holes close on their own. So Kylie began her healing process pretty quickly. The doctors had a lot of hope for her.

I, on the other hand, was a flight risk from the very beginning.

The nurses explained to my parents that I might not survive more than a few days, much less the weeks or months necessary to stabilize me for heart surgery. Plus, it would cost them a lot of money to get me the procedures I'd need.

And truly, my story could have ended there. But God had other plans. Because they didn't even bat an eye. Marsha had survived years with heart problems of her own, and so she had nothing but compassion for her new, blue-faced baby girl.

So little Kylie and (even littler) Karlie began our adventures in a new, loving home.

LIFE AS A TWIN

I always knew I was a twin. From an early age, I always knew I had a constant buddy and protector. People talk about twins being telepathic or connected (and I can't categorically deny anything), but I think at the root of that special connection is an intentional presence. We passed every life milestone together, at the same time, in the same place, and sometimes the same room. Having a twin sibling is like watching yourself grow up. Being a twin meant I would never be alone. Anyone passing us as toddlers, though, wouldn't have known right off that we were twins. Kylie was bigger, stronger, faster, and always feisty. I was tinier, wobblier, and a little less likely to leap off the furniture or take unnecessary risks.

But as mismatched as we looked, the two of us were relentlessly devoted to each other. No one told me bigger stronger kids weren't supposed to play with the little ones—because my sister never showed me otherwise. It actually took a while for me to realize that I was any different, even though no other kids I knew had to sit down every few seconds to breathe or had medical scars down their chests.

And those procedures did come quickly.

At five months old, Mom and Dad took us from Silverton back to Dallas Children's Medical Center in Dallas for my Pulmonary Banding surgery. Kylie and I chilled all the way in our matching car seats. A pulmonary banding is pretty much what it sounds like. The surgeon takes the baby's pulmonary artery, the one from the heart to the lungs, and tightens it with a sort of string. Otherwise, the lungs are being flooded with more blue blood than they can handle. The doctors made an incision under my right breast bone, wrapped the artery, and just like that, I had my very first heart surgery under my very small belt.

Soon visits to unpleasant hospitals were a regular part of my life. The antiseptic smell, the slaps of latex, and long, white hallways are branded in my brain. It was certainly nothing like home. Mom always kept it cozy, warm, and as far from feeling like a hospital room as she could.

When her girlhood cancer left her weak, she had learned how to sew and knit. And she never stopped. Everything we owned, it seemed, was something Mom made with her hands. Clothes, curtains, decorations—she would make gifts for sick friends, neighborhood kids, and always her two favorite girls.

Mom dressed us in the exact same outfits almost daily. If we did wear different things, it was just different colors. Even into our thirties we shopped similar styles—matching on purpose so many times, but sometimes just by accident.

"KylieKarlie!"

That's how mom called us to dinner most of the time, or whenever she found one of our messes. On more than one occasion, our parents found "Karlie did this" or "Kylie did this" written on the wall.

Of course, Mom and Dad knew better.

By the time she was one year old, Kylie was already wobbling and walking through the house. She was the adventurer who may have pulled down a doily or two. But for all the exploring, she soon realized a recurring story—her twin sis couldn't keep up.

My body moved slower. Do you remember those old big boxes that diapers used to come in? We always had the green Huggies ones that had a large hole on the top and opened from that. Well, Mom or Granny would set me down in the box—and Kylie would push me around in the box so I could follow wherever she went.

My lungs were still fighting to support my legs, so walking came slowly. Well, that wasn't going to fly; Kylie needed an adventure buddy. That feeling of inclusion, that someone *wanted* me with them, really caused us to connect deeper.

Honestly, it would have been normal for a sister to resent the other one for getting so much attention—even for life-threatening medical conditions. And sometimes she did try to see what all the fuss was about. Like the time Mom found Kylie under the kitchen cabinets with a familiar bottle. She read the label: Lanoxin, my heart medicine! I can still remember the sickly taste. Yuck!

Mom and Dad rushed Kylie to Lockney to the emergency clinic. But back in those days, they didn't just pump your stomach—not in Lockney anyways. So, Dad had to hold toddler Kylie down so they could feed her charcoal. By the end, it was all over him, the doctors, and the ceilings. Needless to say, Kylie left my Lanoxin alone after that. Being the patient wasn't quite her style. She would rather be the nurse.

Kylie treated each of my limitations as an opportunity. After my Fontan surgery at five years old, I couldn't even walk one hundred feet without getting nauseous. I certainly didn't fit into the Huggies box anymore. But Kylie wouldn't leave me behind, so she upgraded my ride to a bright red wagon. Anytime I just couldn't keep up, Kylie would have me jump in as she pulled, my friend Kurby pushed—and suddenly I was moving just as fast as everyone else. I remember our wagon going down the sidewalk to the school gym for a pep rally. The wheels bumped on every sidewalk crack, but I felt like a Texas pageant queen riding along in her Cadillac.

The constant exhaustion still took a toll, however. In Mrs. Bean's second grade class, I had a little green fan clipped to my little desk and a pile of Hi-C juice boxes underneath. No one else got to have drinks at their desks.

Unfortunately, by the end of the day, I would have thrown up every orange drop. Recess was always hit or miss, because getting overheated made me sick. No one expected me to join the kickball group, or race them to the swings. But that was just the norm for me.

When the nausea got too bad, I got to call home. Mom tucked me and a 3-liter bottle of 7UP into my yellow-gold daybed, the one matching Kylie's down the hall. (We used to be in bunk beds together, until the day she climbed up to the top bunk, leaped onto the still-moving ceiling fan, and yanked it out of the ceiling.)

Dad lent me an old cassette player. It was one of those thin-looking ones with a tape on the right and left side. On each side, I put a Garth Brooks cassette. I might be so sick that I was barely moving, with a cold washrag on my forehead to ease the pain, but when Garth crooned *I've got friends in low places,* I'd forget my problems for just a second.

OFF TO NEVERLAND

My childhood was far from normal, but it was normal to me. Kylie made it so.

I have no idea what it's like to play tag or anything else that requires a lot of physical activity. In elementary school, when everyone went to P.E. class, I went to the nurse, Mrs. Pinkerton's office, to sleep. Sometimes I overslept, but they would just let me rest.

The whole school knew my story.

As the tiniest kid in our grade—always—I was a prime candidate for bullies to pick on me. But no one ever did. Because everyone knew if they were to mess with me, they would have to answer to Kylie.

Kylie took P.E., played basketball, and excelled in every active pursuit. As she grew taller and stronger, we looked less and less alike. Our personalities formed differently, too. Her tenacious, spontaneous spirit complemented my more cautious, thoughtful nature.

In 1990, *the* movie in our house was Disney's *Peter Pan*. Oh my gosh, Kylie *loved* it! Peter was fun and active and never had to grow up. If something bad happened, he could always take off and fly away. Thanks to Peter Pan's influence, Kylie was always trying to fly.

One day, she got on top of our red couch, scooted out to the end of the thick arm, and leaped off, saying, "Come fly with me, Karlie!"

I was not as strong or confident as her, and I was scared. But her boldness at least got me to the top of the couch.

She looked up at me after she'd stuck her landing: "Now... JUMP!"

"No..."

"Do it, you got it!"

"Uh-uh."

Always my encourager, Kylie thought she would give me a little help to "fly." So, she reached up and pulled me off that arm of the couch—and when I fell, my right leg broke in two places!

I don't remember the pain, but I do remember the bright pink cast and the little brown heel they put on the bottom so I could hobble around.

When you get down to it, there's no reason I should have lived past birth, much less after everything that else that would happen to me. Still, I've never been afraid that I was going to die.

Pain and weakness were both something I'd always known and something we were always trying to mediate.

But even when my differences set me apart from my sister, my friends, and most of my family, they also brought me close to the people who truly loved me the most. Even when they were far from my body, their love closed in around my three-chambered heart.

CHAPTER THREE

I Lift My Eyes to the Hills

Silverton, Texas—1995

THE BROWNING TEXAS GRASS CRINCH-CRUNCHED under my Skechers. Some counties had the funds for fancy track turf, but in Silverton in 1995, the open land behind the school was darn good enough for elementary school Field Day.

For years, the school powers-that-be delighted in this great cultural tradition: pitting schoolkids against one another in games of strength and agility. Back then, there were no participation ribbons, no stickers for trying, just good ole, free-market, American competition.

Field Day was a special event for me. My classmates knew I didn't run around at recess and took a nap instead of P.E. class. But I *could* run a three-leg race. I never decided what to do or not do based on other people's reactions. No one ever told me that—standing a head shorter with only three-fourths of a working heart—I had more reason to complain than anybody else. My body told me what I could and couldn't do.

And on field day I told myself, *We're gonna run in a three-leg race.*

I tried to hold my balance while my friend Kurby held her ankle against mine and tied them together.

"Kurby, not so tight!"

She looked up at me and scrunched her nose with all the disgust an 11-year-old could muster. "Karlie, it's gotta be tight or you'll wobble."

"Don't break my ankle…."

"Stop moving it around! One second. *There.*"

My best friend finished tying the fabric scrap and slowly leaned back up. Her sturdy 11-year old legs came all the way up to my belly-button. She looked down with pride at her accomplishment. I was scanning the kids in our vicinity, "You think Kylie will come watch?"

My sister excelled at sports and had already signed up for several field events.

"She'll show," said Kurby, always the encourager.

Kurby liked to say I was her "first friend." And, next to Kylie, Kurby was mine. She's one of those best friends you never went looking for. She found you. She settled into my young life before I even knew to be nervous that someone could get up and walk away.

She never judged me—nor anyone else. She never looked at me like I was different. She just knew I needed a little extra help. She always waited behind for me to walk a little slower than the crowd, and piggy-backed me when I needed it. We could be the last ones to get where we were going, but it wouldn't bother her. And when you never had to earn someone's love, you can't very well be afraid of how you might lose it.

We both knew I wasn't the fastest or the strongest. I couldn't run with the other girls and boys at recess. (Even a light jog could wind me.) But you would have thought I was Usain Bolt when you saw how fast Kurby volunteered to be my racing partner.

Every. Single. Time.

"We're gonna do so great! Let's practice."

We wove our arms around each other, repeating with each step, "Left... right... left, right...." Giggling as we gained speed, Kurby and I began to weave through clumps of other kids. A teacher with a bullhorn called across the field, *Fifth-grade girls to the starting line. Three-legged race girls to the line.*

I fake shrieked, "Wahhhh! Let's go. They can't start without us."

We hobbled up to the starting line, a piece of colored yarn from Mrs. Morrison's kindergarten classroom stretched between two discarded shoes. My little heart was already bump-bump-bumping in anticipation. In those moments, I forgot I was any different from the other kids. *Three-chambered-heart who?* But as the voice on the bullhorn shouted "Go!" and the other pairs of girls scrambled off, my chest tightened. "Slow, slow, slow," I squeezed Kurby's arm. Our pace trailed so I could catch a deliberate breath. With the blood pounding just barely behind my temples, suddenly Kurby pointed down the raceway and yelled, "Heyyyy Kylie!"

I craned my neck to look for her in the crowd of other kids. I knew she'd be wearing the same t-shirt and capri pants as me.

"Karlie, left foot first, okay?"

"Okay."

One step at a time we made our way across the sun-cooked Texas grass to the finish line, (also a piece of yarn) dead last, but still arm-in-arm. We were immediately bear-hugged by a brunette in the matching t-shirt and capri pants. The three of us giggle-screamed until a teacher shushed at us. "Kylie, did you see me? Did you see us go?"

Kylie's face was splotchy red from her own races, "Yeah! You did so great. Like, *really* great. I just did the tug-of-war, and we *totally* beat the boys."

"I bet you beat 'em good."

"So good!"

"Maybe we'll do the tug-of-war together next time?"

Kylie looked thoughtful for a minute. "Yeah. You could be our anchor. With all the snacks you eat, the other team would never move you." At that, Kurby burst out laughing.

Later Kylie and I sat next to each other while our neighbor drove us home, waiting for the familiar turn onto our road. I flipped around and squeezed my face into the small crack between the fake leather seat

"Our stop," Kylie poked me and I swung around. She hopped out of the car first, then turned to hold my hand as I stepped out.

Snuggling into our old red couch, I couldn't wait for Mom to get home so I could tell her about my race. It wasn't usual for us to not know where Mom was, but, then again, she was always ready to help someone out impromptu.

When she finally walked in the front door, I forgot all about the race. She looked like a movie star. I had never seen her in makeup like that. Her soft black hair was done up in curls. Kylie did a double-take too when she came into the living room. Mom handed us a few pictures she had taken.

"Mom, you are *beautiful!*" I emphasized the word so there would be no doubt in her mind. "So beautiful!" Kylie added. We knew she was the most beautiful mom in the world. She hushed us a little, but her soft smile betrayed an inner excitement. As we all went into the kitchen to help with dinner and finally share our Olympian achievements, little did I know that those pictures would be the last ones taken of her.

THE GOOD, THE BAD, AND THE BLESSING

Did you know congenital conditions are mentioned in the Bible? In his Gospel, John describes how some people came to Jesus with an important question. They saw a man who had been blind since birth. His disciples asked why he was born that way. Was it a punishment for his parents' sin? Or his own? Jesus' response surprised them: "Neither this man nor his parents sinned," said Jesus, "but this happened so that the works of God might be displayed in him." (John 9:3)

There's a temptation to look at the sufferers of pain or physical brokenness and assume they must have done something wrong, or that God must have turned His back on the sufferer. But time and time again, both in the Scriptures and in our day, we see that God comes *close* to the sick and suffering. He *longs* to comfort and make His presence known. He doesn't author evil or pain, but in love and power can turn a hard situation into a gift richer than we could imagine.

The world tells us *comfort is good. Discomfort is bad. Abundance is good. Lack is bad.* And while I will not say that being poor and in pain is a good thing in itself, I believe our definition—at least my definition—of *good* or *blessing* may need to change. Most of my "good days" are also days where I forget where the good comes from. When I'm comfortable, I don't always lift my eyes to the hills to see where my help comes from. There is something ironically beautiful about the way our painful circumstances can do the *most* to bring us into the loving presence of a Good Father.ˣ

But do hear me say this: Pain is hard. Pain should be lamented. Addiction, grief, brokenness, and separation is not what God wants for His children. Sin affects entire family and community systems. Billie Holiday once said about her drug addiction, "A habit is no private hell." And my birth mother's habits surely spilled their consequences onto her unborn children.

Maybe if my birth mother hadn't littered her pregnancy with drug abuse and alcohol, I would have a full, healthy body.

Maybe my twin sister wouldn't have been born with a hole in her heart wall.

Maybe we wouldn't have had to deal with the unresolved frustration or the unanswered questions.

But because of my birth mother's condition, she decided to place us with another family, with a mother who wanted us badly, who had a painful past which gave her empathy for other sick children.

Of course, Mom didn't *have* to adopt two little girls with heart defects. She and Dad could have waited. They had every excuse. After her diagnosis with Non-Hodgkin's Lymphoma—at only seventeen—she immediately began radiation and chemo. When her sister and mother took turns driving back and forth for her treatments, everyone braced for the trip back because Mom was always violently ill all the way home. But she never complained.

Later that year she met a roguish redhead named Steve. The youngest of seven siblings, his story had been rough, too. After a childhood working his hands to the bone on the family farm, he had exploded into teenage independence. He was the guy who drank, partied, and answered to no one—that is until he met the charming Marsha. Her kind determination and steadfast perseverance through suffering cut him to the core. This was a woman worth fighting for, someone worth putting away the bottles and cigarettes.

They married at the age of eighteen after her chemo was done. One of Mom's friends sold them a tiny three-bedroom, two-bathroom house in Silverton, Texas for $7,000. Mom couldn't work a normal 9-to-5 job because she was so sick and weak. But she sure as heck wasn't going to sit still doing nothing. So Mom sewed. She sewed for the whole town. Literally. She and Dad were poor, but they were happy.

She could have leaned on her sickness as a reason to look for healthy children, ones who could take care of *her* and wouldn't need extra money and care.

Instead, my mother looked at us through the glass and said, "I want those babies!" She took those babies and told them about a God who loved, healed, and held us in the hurt that hadn't passed yet. She taught us to trust that God brings the hurting together to love each other. He brings us through. Her faith reminded her that we love because we have first been loved. Her love showed us how to care for people *because* we have been cared for.

Every year we showed up at VBS at our tiny First Baptist Church in Silverton. For anyone who has never experienced small-town VBS, it's part family reunion, part Sunday school, part theater, and part pint-sized revival. The last day was usually an altar call. I was too nervous to walk down to the front, but Kylie did. She and another girl were bawling. We all gave our lives to Christ. It was truly childlike faith, and even past the tears that dried or the emotions that passed, a seed planted in my heart, slowly growing, budding, waiting to bloom.

Another key event in my spiritual growth came as a result of not being able to go to our church camp activity. "Girls in Action" or GA camp was a camp for girls through our church. Kylie and I were about seven the first time our church sent girls to the camp a few hours away. Because of my health, I didn't get to go. Instead, Mom and Dad sent me to Heart Camp! The Dallas Children's Medical Center (where I had already had my first three surgeries) put on a camp where sick kids get to experience things as normal children. Instead of normal camp counselors, all the staff are doctors, nurses, and volunteers from the hospital.

I remember getting on the bus at the hospital and heading to Meridian, Texas, where the camp was. Mom was nervous that I was by myself and didn't know anyone. Kylie was too healthy to attend. But I ended up meeting a girl right before we got on the bus named Kelly. I remember her blonde hair to this day. We sat together the whole way and even shared the same cabin! All the kids there were like me. Sick and tired. But we got to do everything normal kids would do if they attended camp. We rode horses, climbed a rock wall, ziplined—everything.

When I got too tired, the doctors piggy-backed us or pushed us in wheelchairs. I ended up going twice and still remember it vividly to this day. Three years later, when Kylie and I were ten, Mom and Dad finally let me go to GA Camp with our friends! The only reason they let me go was because Kylie could now tell when I was sick or needed anything. I got to go because she was there to take care of me.

I did things like calligraphy and baking while she went off and did races and stuff like that which would make me tired. Kurby went to the same church as we did, so she was right along beside us the entire way. I'll never forget that "Girls in Action" camp and how it grew my faith in God and my faith in my own abilities and relationships with Kurby and Kylie.

NOVEMBER 15, 1995

"Girls, Betty Nan is going to take y'all up to school, okay?"

I was in the middle of a bowl of cereal. Kylie was reading the back of the box.

"Something going on?" I mumbled through milky flakes.

Mom was calling softly from her new bedroom. "I'm just not feeling good. She might pick you up too." Mom didn't sleep in the master bedroom anymore. Kylie and I didn't know why. Mom and Dad weren't arguing. But nevertheless, Dad had cleared out her sewing room and stuffed a large bed in there, with a foam prop for Mom to sit up and sleep on. We never questioned it. They never offered an explanation.

Betty Nan was a sweet older lady who lived across the street from us. She sometimes substituted at the school, so she would often take us to and from there to help Mom out if she wasn't feeling good and Dad was working. While we waited for her, I gave Kylie a look. She shrugged. Something felt off, but neither of us truly wanted to imagine what.

We went to school and tried to concentrate. But hours before normal pickup, we got called by a teacher to the front office. Betty Nan had arrived. I climbed into her handicapped-equipped van right behind the driver's seat. Kylie sat behind her husband, Spud. He had MS and was in a wheelchair.

"Betty Nan, where's Mom?"

"We're going to see her now."

"But where? Where is she?"

"In Lubbock, honey, we'll see her soon."

You can't fool a girl who grew up visiting doctors. The closest hospital was in Lubbock. Betty Nan must have been driving there fast because we got pulled over by a black and white cop car. *We can't go to jail. We need to go get Mom.* I remember looking up at the cop through the window. *Please, we gotta go.* Whatever Betty Nan said, it was either convincing or worthy of pity, because soon we were back on the road.

We got to Lubbock Hospital and found Granny in the waiting room. If anyone else important was there, I didn't notice them. We ran straight to Granny's lap and stayed there until a nurse called us back. Daddy and Aunt Dorothy were already in the room. Mom was asleep, sitting up. Her face was yellow. I was used to being blue. I never knew peoples' faces could turn that color. Something was on mom's shoulder, I pointed and asked what it was. Aunt Dorothy had pinned an angel pin on her shoulder.

We talked to Mom, but she never responded. I wanted to shout, *Mom, it's us! KylieKarlie! You need to come home with us.* Kylie and I walked back out to the waiting room and I crawled up in Granny's lap. I remember Dad coming in a few minutes later and hitting the door frame and collapsing.

Mom had died. She was only thirty-five. It was as if she had waited until Kylie and I could tell her bye, and then she let go. Adults wouldn't tell us what happened for years. But the truth was that Mom's cancer had come back. Non-Hodgkin's Lymphoma had caused her to develop lupus, and when the cancer came back, her body just couldn't take it. We went to school that day with a mom, and came home without one. We were only eleven years old.

Mom's funeral took place in the same tiny church Kylie and I grew up in. We sat in the same pews we had cried in during VBS. Kylie and I sat side by side, watching the people file in dressed in fancy black clothes. It didn't feel real. I looked down front at the casket. Mom couldn't be in there. She walks around. She hugs us. She doesn't lay around in boxes. She doesn't turn yellow or not respond to "I love you."

My little brain knew how to process a lot of things, like pain and exhaustion and missing out, but I didn't know how death fit in. *Who do you cry to when the person you always cry to is the person you're crying about?* I threw up half-way through. A cousin carried me out.

Kylie and I didn't talk about Mom a lot after that. Dad never brought her up. We really just kept to ourselves. Looking back now, I see we really just held everything inside. Kylie did do one thing special for me that I remember. Every night I would lay in bed with her as she sang one song I would always request. She would sing "Angels Among Us" by Alabama. I don't even know how we came to know that song, but she sang the chorus to me whenever I asked her or needed it.

The pain of those days was intense, but unfortunately the hard times were just beginning.

CHAPTER FOUR

The Anatomy of Grief

E VERYONE DEALS WITH HEARTBREAK DIFFERENTLY. Some people rush to comforting arms. Others draw back into themselves. Many put up walls to keep the pain at bay. Some simply go into survival mode. *Will I live through this pain? Or do I need to get rid of it at all costs?*

But did you know that deep grief can actually rewire our brains?

Loss, like the death of a family member, triggers a trauma response in our bodies. Researchers at the Johns Hopkins University confirmed the validity of "broken heart" syndrome when they discovered that sudden emotional stress can result in severe heart muscle weakness that mimics a heart attack. The researchers found that people may respond to sudden overwhelming emotional stress by releasing large amounts of stress hormones into the bloodstream. These chemicals can be toxic to the heart, effectively stunning the muscles and causing heart attack-like symptoms.[1]

In short, grief can change people in unexpected ways. None of us were the same after my mom's funeral, Dad least of all.

As I opened my eyes to the grey November sunlight, it all felt like a bad dream. For an eleven-year-old child, the fact that time keeps going after the worst day of your life doesn't make any sense. It's an unholy feeling. My thoughts bounced around like popcorn.

No, no, I'm not going to just eat cereal today. You expect me to put on these socks like a regular girl whose mom is still alive?

Grief set in slowly, like coming in from the cold and thawing your hands—they're feeling again. And boy does that hurt. The grief bubbled like nausea in my little stomach. *Could I throw it up? Spit out the sad like I did my orange Hi-C? Who was going to tuck me and my 7UP into bed again?*

Familiar things felt sacrilegious, like shadows of what they used to be. As painful as they were, I knew I didn't

---

[1]   Journal of the American College of Cardiology: *Lazzarino A, et al, "The Association between cortisol response to mental stress and high-sensitivity cardiac troponin T plasma concentration in healthy adults" J Am Coll Cardio 2013*

want them gone. I wanted things back how they were. But deep down, I knew they couldn't be.

Ever? Ever ever? Like forever? Forever didn't make sense to those eleven-year-old girls who had only ever known a small, safe town with Mom and Dad and red wagons. Sure, there were some hospital visits, but always with Mom and Dad. Who wants the reality of forever when that reality punches you in the stomach every morning?

Consciousness reminds you of the hollow feeling in your stomach that hasn't grown back in yet. And how dare it ever grow in! Everything familiar is painful, because the person who shared those memories is gone, so remembering the good means remembering what won't be that good anymore. But somehow we had to go on and make new memories. That's what humans have had to do for thousands of years, and we were no different.

They say you never truly get over grief, you just keep moving forward towards a new normal. Maybe that's why Dad started packing it all up. At first he just boxed the decorations, all the warm touches Mom placed around the house. Then he took down Mom's art, crafts and sewing. Soon he was into her closet, lifting a dozen hangers at once out and onto the bed. Her jewelry, heirlooms, even her 1960s Barbie dolls in their round black case she had kept from childhood. Her class ring with a pink stone and her small delicate wedding ring were boxed up, but not put in the attic to be saved for her little girls. Instead, he gave her trinkets and crafts to women across town. He sold her jewelry to strangers.

It felt like my mom was being erased.

GRIEF BRINGS STRANGE THINGS

Kylie and I were shocked one evening to walk in on him boxing *our* toys. My favorite lamb that had been with me through all three heart surgeries was now gone. Our matching baby dolls, Barbies, and everything were disappearing.

"Daddy, don't put that up," Kylie said, sounding somewhere between annoyed and terrified.

He didn't turn around. "We'll get you new stuff. Better stuff."

"But I like *my* stuff...."

"This isn't time to be selfish," he said with thinly veiled annoyance.

His grownup voice had the weight of someone who *did* know better but somehow didn't care. Something still felt wrong. I stayed a few feet back from their conversation. Kylie was always better at conflict.

"Why all of it? Can I keep just—just that one?"

"Kylie Re Nee', you won't speak to me in that tone. Go to the living room!" We held hands and left together. Kylie yanked me down the hallway. The confused look I shot her said, *Is this normal? Does everyone have to get rid of their toys after someone dies?* It did seem selfish to complain. To a kid growing up in the Bible belt, manners and respect were everything. Maybe our toys *were* a problem. But then again, two eleven-year-olds were no match for the crushing weight of grief.

Sometimes grief makes you explode. Sometimes you implode. Grief doesn't take your feelings into account. Not even the feelings of your twin daughters. And, y'all, I lived through it, and can tell you *that's hard.*

Any object that reminded him of life with Mom disappeared. The clothes she had sewed for us, the toys they had given us, the furniture they'd picked out together—gone.

Not some, not most, *everything.*

Pretty soon almost everyone in Silverton had a piece of our mother, everyone except us. You would have never known a loving family had once lived in that 600-square-foot house. With Mom no longer there, it certainly didn't feel like home.

A deep loneliness seemed to have opened in my dad's heart. I wondered if it had literally been broken in two. Maybe it had shrunk down to the size of mine. They say it's one of the most painful things a human can bear, losing a spouse.

But Kylie and I wanted him to know, we wanted to scream it loudly: *We lost Mom, too!* And when he lost himself over Mom's death, it felt like we lost him, too.

With our momma gone, where was the daddy we could cry to? Kylie and I hadn't experienced a family death before, so we didn't know if this was normal. After all traces of her were packed up and removed from the house, he never talked to us about her, not without a lot of pressure. He stopped taking us to the Baptist Church, so we didn't go to any church at all.

In a situation like that, it's easy to believe that you're crazy for feeling grief. After all, it didn't seem like many other people were. Life went on. Did anyone understand?

Dad worked two different jobs in Amarillo. That left us girls to take care of each other most days—and just like she had all our lives, Kylie stepped up to take charge. I was so tired constantly that sometimes she would get me dressed and brush my teeth while I was sitting on the end of my daybed. Kylie always made sure my homework was done and that I was feeling ok. She never left my side during those times. I slept right next to her every night after Mom's death. When I would get really bad abdominal migraines, she always knew what to do. She would get me an ice cold rag and lay it on my head, turn the light out, and try to get the room as dark as she could while I cried myself to sleep. She truly was a mother to me.

At some point Dad went from frantically getting rid of our possessions to a slightly more relaxed style of living. We should have guessed something was in the works, but when you're eleven you don't look for duplicity in people you should be able to trust. He'd halfheartedly reassure us, "Everything's gonna be fine, girls." I didn't believe it, but I hoped he was right.

In February, Dad pulled us out of school again. I half expected to hear that someone else had died. After bringing us to the house, he told each of us to pack a bag (which was easy because we didn't own much anymore). *Maybe he's taking us on vacation?*

Everything we owned fit into our tiny blue Festiva. We weren't going on vacation. We were leaving town. It turned out that during the winter months, Dad had reconnected with an old friend from high school. A lady friend. They were getting married. We were all moving in with her. She lived forty-five minutes away in Pampa, so when we turned out of our small gravel driveway, that's where we were headed.

At that moment, the emptiness of the house was a mercy. It hadn't felt like home in a long time, and what home I'd had seemed to have died with my mom. Still, driving away, not knowing when or if we would be back, made me feel like a weed plucked from the ground. My lifelong roots were dangling, dropping dirt clods everywhere.

Compared to the 600-square-foot Silverton house, the woman my dad married lived in a mansion. The outside looked middle-class inviting, with a brick face, nice lawn, and no chips on the painted window shutters.

The inside was pretty, too. She lived there with her two sons from a previous marriage. One was a little younger than us, and one was a little older. It was an adjustment for sure. The whole younger/older sibling hierarchy never felt applicable to Kylie and me because we were twins. We loved, respected, and supported each other in everything. She was bigger and stronger, so she helped me. Age and gender had no place in our roles.

Suddenly, not only did we have older and younger siblings, we had brothers.

Instead of our sweet momma, we had a woman I'll call Susan.

A "FAIRY TALE" LIFE

Susan didn't stand very tall, but she easily commanded the house. After letting us into the house, she quickly introduced us to our living space—a shared bedroom with a single waterbed. A 2,500-square-foot house, and we had to share a waterbed.

As I said, the house looked pretty from the outside, but looks can be deceiving. In my opinion, Dad mellowed out at Susan's—which means that he didn't sell any more of our things, but he sort of left us on our own emotionally. The following years would become some of the worst for Kylie and me.

The move wasn't just a shock because of the speed of life. The size was crazy different, too. Silverton boasted about 600 citizens in total. In a few years, we would discover that our new middle school class in Pampa had *400 kids*. You might as well have shipped us to New York City! Dad called the school, setting us up in every class together. Over the years, we did meet some good friends. In Silverton all the teachers knew me because they all had known Mom. But in Pampa we were nobody special. And for good measure, underneath the culture shock of a new town simmered life with Susan.

Based on my observations, she seemed to pick on Kylie the most. It hurt me to see my sister—the strong, vivacious, headstrong twin—torn down every day.

Every weekend I could hear the cars pull out of the driveway—our step-brothers headed out on their teen escapades. And at the same time, Susan would *lock our door* from the outside. I know it sounds dramatic, but it's exactly what happened to us. She gave us some cock-and-bull pretense, but every week it was assumed: the boys go out while the girls stay home.

We were outraged, especially Kylie.

One night she decided to give our stepmother a piece of her mind. I looked around the door just in time to see Susan sock Kylie in the face. Her eye stayed blackened for two days, so Dad kept her home from school. Dad didn't seem to challenge any of Susan's rules.

One Friday, when we were sixteen, he did tell us, "Just sneak out the window and push the car down the road."

We never tried it—not that we didn't have friends who would help us. Kylie was well-liked at school, and I was too. But the more pushback Susan felt from us, the worse things seemed to get at home.

I wasn't much of a fighter, so she didn't pick on me much. But fiery Kylie would go *at it* with her. One time in the middle of a fight, Kylie tried to have the last word and retreat up the stairs. I saw Susan hurl the nearest object at her. Later I would listen to my sister rant as we jumped on and off the waterbed. I wanted to support her, and I wished I had the energy to stand up to Susan the way she did. We felt like some sort of *Grimm's Fairy Tale* characters. Where was our courageous prince?

But life goes on.

In May, we enrolled at Pampa Middle School and, thankfully, Dad did take the initiative to call our principal. In Silverton there were only a dozen kids to a class, so Kylie and I took every class together. In Pampa, everyone got different schedules. I'm not sure how things would have gone if she and I had been separated every day. Instead, he called, told the school about my medical conditions and history, and asked to keep us together.

By the grace of God, they said yes.

So we spent our school days—the only Susan-free hours—together, every class except for P.E. Kylie went to basketball practice, and I went to choir. Kylie got the black eyes, the shouting matches, the dirty looks. I had Kylie's back. Injustice is a grief all its own, and while it affects us differently than death, it chips away at us just as steadily.

Those years were tough, but they did something you wouldn't have thought possible—they made two already joined-at-the-hip sisters closer than ever before, and that bond deepened to the point where I thought nothing could break us apart.

CHAPTER FIVE

Shaken Securities

I DON'T KNOW WHAT KYLIE AND I would have done without each other during those years in Pampa. The only times we felt truly safe was in class together, or in our room, after everyone else in the house fell asleep. When Kylie turned in her sleep, the soft movement would send me bobbing on the waterbed. I would strain my ears to hear what was happening out into the hallway, praying for silence.

In middle school, Kylie took a job at Sonic. Well, more accurately, Susan put her up to it in my opinion. In some ways, Kylie appreciated any excuse to be out of that house. I sure missed her, but was excited that one of us could be out there in the "real world." It had to be different than what I experienced. And a job meant money—and money meant independence!

Or so we thought.

Payday came for Kylie a couple weeks later. We had talked late into the night about what she could do with her new income. Movie tickets, clothes? How much did cars cost? *At least a thousand dollars probably.* Maybe the reason we had to stay in each weekend was because we couldn't support ourselves yet. This revenue stream could change our entire social lives.

Kylie strutted through the front door with pride. She held her first check and tips she had earned in a white-knuckled pinch, like it could fly away. I couldn't hold back the pride in my smile. "You're a real working girl, Kylie! Lemme see!"

She raised her eyebrows in fake modesty. "Oh, this? Already forgot about it."

I pulled her arm down to get a look. The cursive was so fancy: "Pay to the order of: Kylie Green."

We both startled as Susan came around the corner. She didn't seem as excited. In a very matter-of-fact voice she said, "Hand that here." I scrunched my eyes and looked back and forth between the staredown happening between Susan and my sister.

"Kylie, you know that's for the family."

"But... but it says her name." The words sounded bolder in my head.

Kylie rolled her eyes, but then looked resigned. From my conversations with Kylie, I knew Susan would go on to take every single check my sister brought home. Family support? Maybe she expected something more from her stepchildren because she graced us with a big house. *You can have it all back,* I thought. Because without a doubt, Kylie and I both would have traded it all—house, waterbed, paychecks—to be back in that 600-square-foot Silverton bungalow with our mom.

TAKING A TOLL

As the months passed, the disappointment took an even greater toll, especially on Kylie. She had so much spunk. In our younger years that spunk had made her the best protector, the best encourager, the best friend anyone could ask for.

In Pampa, her spunk made her a target.

Kylie's tenacity had been the rock my arms clung to for so many years. It felt like Dad had backed away from us emotionally. He hadn't taken us to church since Mom passed. And good luck trying to get there by ourselves. God became an idea of hope, but one that floated high above me. No one continued to remind us of the loving relationship God wanted to have with me. That he saw past my weakness, shortcomings, and mistakes. I heard that God was like a father, but one who comes close to you when you're sad. He protects you when you're being hurt. This was a far cry from what I was experiencing with my own father.

Thankfully, God stayed close to us, even when we didn't think we were close to Him. He protected my sister and me in ways we never realized until years later. Even in the depths of our sadness and frustration, He was there.

In times of stress, our bodies will eat away at anything extra, shrinking us down to the essentials of life. But if hard times continue, and we don't feed or nurture it, our body will begin to tear away at its own foundations—even its own heart. During that time in Pampa, both Kylie and I had our foundations shaken. Over and over. The pain ate away at her soul.

When we were fifteen, she decided that the pain was too much—I didn't know this happened until years later, but she took a bottle of pills to try and end it all. Thank God, she survived.

But there was no time to waste. As soon as she recovered, we started talking about high school graduation. That would be our real ticket out.

With her grades, and if she really applied herself, she could graduate five months early. Kylie wanted to get a college education, so she set her sights on Texas Tech—and she wanted me to come with her! Because of my health, the stress of college life didn't quite appeal to me as it did to her. But, by gosh, if one of us was going to get out, both of us were.

In December 2001, we both graduated, packed (quickly), left Dad—he and Susan had divorced by that time—and headed for Lubbock, TX.

This would be the first home Kylie and I had absolute control over. We could decorate how we wanted, go in and out when we wanted, eat whatever we wanted. The freedom was overwhelming at first. My excitement, however, surpassed any fears. We spent the first night in our new apartment setting up the few pieces of furniture, and eating food while we sat on the ground. It felt right, like we were adventuring for real now. And everything was about to take a shocking twist. Kylie went straight to the financial aid office on her first day at a new school after transferring from Tech to finish her degree. She and I had high hopes that she could qualify for substantial help. But arriving at the door, she looked twice at the name on the office door. *No, no, no!* There was no way; there had to be two of them.

When she walked in, her worst fear was confirmed. Small, blonde, and with a sickening pep in her voice, the woman took a moment before looking up, "Hello. Please come in, I'm your advisor—why, hello Kylie."

"Shit." Kylie's heart sank—in some kind of crazy stroke of bad luck, her financial advisor was none other than Susan.

At home I got an earful. Kylie paced the apartment in a fury. I sat at the kitchen table, trying to make sense of what was happening.

"I could not believe it. In Lubbock? Why is she in Lubbock? What are the odds?"

I sighed. "Our family isn't really great with odds."

"Karlie, this was a new life. Our new start. That woman is going to give me—give us—hell all over again."

"I don't know. This is her job. Maybe she isn't allowed—"

Kylie stopped pacing and looked at me head-on. "She's already doing it."

Kylie fought tooth and nail for any financial help, and at every turn any aid was delayed. Like the Israelites after Egypt, I wondered, *God, what is going on? I thought this was our escape?* We had escaped captivity, only to run smack into the Dead Sea.

PLEASE, NOT TODAY!

Then one day I walked past Kylie's door and saw it was shut. We rarely shut our doors. I reached for the handle. Locked. A little ball of heat swirled in my stomach. I rattled the knob, "Kylie? You okay?"

Silence. Then, "Yeah. I'm resting."

"Can I come in and talk?"

"I'm really, really tired."

The changes got worse. Kylie started staying out later. She was well-liked, as always, but her friends seemed...

different now. We had fewer and fewer carefree talks. I discovered that she had started pawning things at the local shop. My sister felt somewhere far, far away.

Somehow she kept up grades, and kept passing classes. So I felt kind of silly. *Maybe I'm overreacting?* But her emotions seemed to swing back and forth. One night she was the life of the party. Another her door was locked again. I started to suspect the truth and finally called Dad. I could barely get out the words. What if speaking them made it even more real? And for a long time afterwards I blamed myself. If I would have told him sooner, would she have gotten so bad?

It never entered my mind that Kylie could get sicker than me. In my mind my sister equaled perfect health, of body, mind, and spirit. If any of us were supposed to be in the hospital, it was always me. Her role was elsewhere. Mom, Pampa, Susan, Dad, school. She had carried it so strongly, or so I thought. But we were about to learn the cost.

When everything came crashing down, it felt like a horrific dream.

It was late 2003, and she had almost made it through college. The pain in her chest took us by surprise. If it had been me, of course we would have known exactly which doctors to go to, exactly what medications were best, and who would take care of me. But Kylie went downhill so fast, we didn't have time to make those plans.

Dad rushed into town to pick her up. He didn't know where to go. Everyone he reached out to turned him down. Too busy. Call back. Wait list.

Kylie was very thin and very sick. The doctors she did manage to see had revealed she had had an infection in her Aortic Valve. We could all tell that she was dying. She didn't have time for a waitlist. So Dad drove her all over the state of Texas, from Houston to Austin, trying to get her help. He called our congressman. He called the governor.

I hadn't seen my father so invested in years. He did everything he could to save Kylie's life. Yet it seemed no one my dad reached out to even tried to help him.

I truly believe that God sent the final name to Dad. Our mother had died eight years previously, and Dad had tried to erase everything connected to her death from his life. But in that moment, with Kylie dying in the backseat, he picked up the phone one more time.

"Hello. This is Steve Green. Yes. Well, doctor, you, um, well you were my wife's cardiologist back in…." He paused, and looked surprised. "You *do* remember Marsha?" Of course, that didn't surprise me at all. Even on her sick days, my mother was a personality you didn't forget.

"Thank you, thank you so much, sir. Yes. Goodbye." He told me that the doctor had retired, *but* he did have an old partner, a cardiologist in Lubbock who could take my sister's case. I prayed we weren't too late.

Kylie went into immediate heart surgery. It felt strange to watch someone else I loved wheeled off on a bed. The doctors found that infection had set in. A vegetative growth had attached to her aorta and was poisoning her blood. She came out, alive, but in tough shape. I rushed—as fast as I could rush—into her room and held back a gasp. Her chest was wide open. Straight up blood, tape, and gauze. The trauma had left her body too swollen to be sewn up yet.

That night, Dad, some other family and I stayed in a nearby hotel while she recovered. But in the middle of the night, I woke up violently. My chest had tightened. I couldn't breathe. *Not now, please not now.* Dad wanted to call the ambulance, but I told them no. This felt different. I struggled for breath, but the strangest sense made me feel like everything was going to be okay.

When we came back to hospital for visiting hours, the doctors told Dad that Kylie coded in the middle of the night. She had nearly died, but pulled through. Now, I'm not very superstitious. But that wouldn't have been the first time Kylie and I had shared moments of pain. I was just thankful she had made it another day.

Because of the infection, Kylie's aortic valve had to be replaced. Patients get to choose between two options: a mechanical valve that stays in forever, or a pig valve that has to be replaced every decade. A lot of people choose the mechanical option, but Kylie had a special dream. Just like our mother, she wanted children so badly. With a mechanical pump and the lifelong medication that comes with it, Kylie's body would never be able to get pregnant. That potential future broke her heart. So despite our concerns, she asked for the pig valve.

By that time, Kylie had begun seeing a man named Derrick she had met at Texas Tech. He had seen her through the challenges she faced in college, her infection, and into her recovery. I liked Derrick. He was kind, funny, and could keep up with Kylie's tenacious spirit.

He helped the family wheel her out of the hospital in 2004. She looked a sight with IVs sticking out, and the scar across her chest. But by the grace of God she came home. Well, not home in Lubbock. Dad offered us space back in Pampa. And with both of us girls in delicate condition, we didn't refuse.

ROCKED MY WORLD

Once she recovered from heart surgery, Kylie went back to school at West Texas AMU near Amarillo. Derrick's family lived in Amarillo so they saw each other a lot, and even got matching finance degrees. (Cute, right?) Soon all of us began getting used to the new season of healing.

I got a job in Amarillo and began leaning into more independence. I had taken a nine-month course to be a pharmacy technician and passed the state exam before the class even finished. I started working at Eckerd's

Pharmacy for a little over minimum wage. It wasn't much, but I was doing it on my own.

I thought I had experienced my share of pain and fear in life. But nothing had prepared me for seeing my twin sister in that hospital bed. My foundation had been rocked. But with the pain came a humbling lesson. Even the people we look up to most can fall, sometimes hard. Everyone is fallible. But unconditional love shows up anyway.

Life can and will change up on you in a heartbeat. It sure has changed on me. But one thing stays the same. God has never left me alone, because He never leaves His children.

I think about the Israelites. They were probably the most complaining, ungrateful, fallible group of people. But God freed them from captivity. Even when they complained again, he brought them through the Red Sea. He gave them Manna for their hunger, water for their thirst. He had every reason to give up on them. But he stayed faithful—not because of who they were, but because of who *he* is—and brought them to the Promised Land.

Through it all, even when it wasn't always clear to me, God's love sustained me.

CHAPTER SIX

Kissin' Frogs

ID YOU EVER PLAY THE game M.A.S.H. as a kid? It's the one where you and a few good friends figure out if you'll live in a mansion or a shack. If you'll have two kids or thirty-two. And, of course, who's going to marry Brad Pitt.

Did you ever wonder about your future spouse? Did you imagine a big, fancy wedding or monograms or baby names? When you're dreaming as a kid, anything is possible. At least, that's what I assume is true for most people.

For me, girlhood unfolded without those thoughts. Instead, my future held a few hard truths. I would battle physical limitations my entire life. I would learn to live with different expectations. I could never have my own children. And without the ability to have kids, I probably wouldn't have a husband. Who would choose to marry me over any other "fully-functioning" woman? At least that's how the script went in my head.

Other women could create a lineage. I was just me.

Since the beginning, that had been my understanding. And, honestly, because I hadn't had the time to hope for anything different, it was just my normal.

But that also meant I could focus on other priorities— and my sister's growing family felt practically like my own.

She and Derrick had their son Keegan Dayne Collins in 2008. We were all overjoyed, but no one more than Kylie. She embodied our mother's wholehearted desire for children. This healthy birth cemented in her mind that the pig valve had been the right decision. And I couldn't argue with her.

If it weren't for that pig valve, we never would have welcomed beautiful Keegan into the family. I looked at them and a thought wandered into my head, harmless and nonchalant, but clear, "Is that really not in my future?" After all, they told Mom she would never have children. She still found Dad. She still found us. If our lives really were like a funky fairy tale, did I have a dashing prince on the way, too?

For the most part, I only found frogs.

FINDING LOVE IN HAWAII

It's a scary thing, maneuvering the dating world, especially as a short little thing who can't exactly sprint away if a guy gets weird. I did have some boyfriends, each one disappointing. Most of them cheated on me. None of them made me feel safe, trusting, or unconditionally valued. All the while, Kylie had a new group of people who needed her. A husband, a child, and prayers for a second one.

As Kylie moved into a new role of motherhood, our sisterhood started to change. It wasn't the dark, scary feeling I had in Lubbock. But we weren't each other's first priority. And for girls who hadn't needed anyone but each other for over twenty-four years, the shift took some adjustment.

To be candid, sometimes the shifting felt more like drifting.

In May 2009, I had the blood clot scare that I shared about in the first chapter, the one that almost canceled my highly-awaited trip to Hawaii. Sometimes I wonder what would be different now if the doctors had shut me down. No flying. No Hawaii. Oh, I sure would have thrown a hissy fit. But sometimes the things we *think* we can't do without, aren't truly as glittering as they appear.

My girlfriends and I had planned the trip to see a good friend of ours from high school. He was a proud member of the U.S. Navy and stationed in Pearl Harbor. He had let us know that we were welcome to visit anytime and promised to show us all the best spots. By the time I took that trip to the hospital for the first clot, everything was paid for and ready to go. It felt like we just couldn't *not go*.

We made it to the island, and oh, it was gorgeous as all get-out! Perfect warm winds, swaying tropical trees, and vibrant colors that seemed realer than real. I couldn't wait to explore. That first day, our friend planned to take us sight-seeing and brought someone I'd never met: "Karlie, this is my best friend." I had to crane my head back to see all 6'2" of him. "He's Navy with me."

With a charming smile, the newly introduced guy (I'll call him Mike) held out a hand to shake. I was hooked.

We clicked right off the bat. Every day of that vacation we found some way to see each other. Talking felt just so easy. He told me he was going through a divorce and had a son back in Ohio. He seemed different than other guys I'd dated. Instead of pushing to go out and drink at night, he would ask me to get ice cream. Or walk on the beach. He also had an advantage because I trusted my other friend's judgment.

Mike didn't appear phased by my physical condition or limitations. All of the fears, all of the scripts I had repeated to myself: *No one is going to want you. You're better off alone. No one wants a sick, slow, small, infertile…* The voices just stopped. I felt so safe and taken care of.

It was during those last days in Hawaii that my ankles began to swell. Everything went blurry. But I tried to pull it together so Mike and I could enjoy a little more time together. I didn't want to leave him.

Even after I left, Mike and I stayed in contact. Even through my emergency trip to Houston, the heart and lung clot, and the weeks of in-patient care. After my clot scare, Mike and I were in contact constantly.

He couldn't visit because of being out to sea so much. And so during those times he was away, I finally flexed my daydreaming muscles. I woke up every hope and dream that the younger Karlie had put away.

The next four months flew by in a whirlwind of giddy phone calls, visits, and life planning. We had met in April, my surgery happened in early May, and before Fall, Mike proposed. Everything was falling into place. Mike flew me, all my belongings—even my dog—out to be with him in Hawaii.

We had a quick ceremony in Hawaii with just us two, God and a judge. He rented us a beautiful house! For once, the man in my life was actively providing for my needs. It was all too amazing. Too good to be true.

What I didn't plan for was Kylie's reaction. After hearing about my upcoming move, she was devastated. Having a new family was one thing. But shooting off five thousand miles away? Across three time zones and a whole ocean? The speed of my relationship unnerved her a little, as well. But, even as sad as she felt, Kylie didn't ask me to stay. She saw me so swept off my feet, finally living out a dream I'd had since childhood. She tried to support me in spite of her worries.

But once we boarded the plane and left for good, that's when it hit home for both of us. We had been all the other had for so long. And now both of us were across the world from each other, trying to live out a new normal with new relationships, homes, and lives.

We tried to Facetime as much as possible, but then the calls got fewer and farther between. Eventually, they stopped. I understood she felt abandoned. But isn't this what we were supposed to do? Grow apart? Build our own families?

But after sharing so much for so many years, five-thousand miles *was* quite a long way—our twin senses were going haywire. In fact, when I look at pictures from those months, I can see that my hair had started falling out. The physical and emotional separation was taking an emotional *and* physical toll. I consoled myself with the fact that I had found my fairytale love story. It would all be worth the pain.

Unfortunately, the pain hadn't even really begun.

BROKEN TRUST

It always feels like the most earth-shattering news comes on a regular Tuesday. Your reality turns upside down in a second. But it's still Tuesday.

Two years into marriage, Mike and I had moved to Rio Rancho, New Mexico. (It wasn't Hawaii, but at least it was still warm.) He'd left the Navy to take a great job with a computer company. Sometimes his hours were long, but I was proud of the hard work he seemed to have put into this new career. Until that regular old Tuesday.

That was the night I got a strange Facebook message from a woman I didn't know. It was the kind of message that turns your insides upside-down.

I read and re-read the message to be sure it wasn't spam. But it was real. I was nearly sick. This woman said she knew Mike from Hawaii. Not only that, she claimed she had carried on an affair with him, meeting up together any time I came home to visit family. And it had been happening since the very beginning of our marriage.

"He told me he was single and he shipped you back to Texas." *Shipped me back? Like a pair of pants he was returning? I'm his wife. Till death do us part. Right?*

I tried to stifle the growing panic. This man loved me. At least, I'd always believed so. I looked over at his computer. *No, don't be the crazy one.* But who could help it? I opened the laptop and started scrolling. Emails, texts, browser history, I read it all.

No. No... NO!

I rolled over onto the floor, groaning. It was all there. Apparently, Mike hadn't just been cheating with this woman. But with multiple women.

I don't remember how long I searched before finding the Craigslist ad. That one stabbed me in the gut. I didn't even know what all the words meant... but clearly, he hadn't been cheating with just women.

We'd traveled together. We'd explored. We'd dreamed. *I had trusted him.* With my health situation, I couldn't even take penicillin. If an STD had transferred... I was terrified of the consequences.

The only thing I knew to do was pick up my cell phone and dial Kylie.

I whispered, "Don't tell Dad, but I just found out Mike has been cheating on me and...." No one else knew—who would believe me? But I told her everything. "I can't believe it, there's so much... oh my gosh, what am I going to do?"

She responded immediately, "I'm coming to get you."

Tears welled up and spilled down my cheeks. Even after so long apart, she was still coming. Later, there was a knock at the door. I opened it, expecting to rush into Kylie's arms. But it was my dad along with Kylie.

"Kylie! I told you not to tell him!"

"Sorry," she half winked and then hugged me tight.

They packed up my stuff, and I left right then and there. The first thing we did back in Amarillo was visit Kylie's doctor. I was totally done. Exhausted. So I told him straight, "If I have something or I'm dying, call Kylie cause I don't want to hear it."

Thank God, every test came back negative.

After the immediate fear went down, the rest of the grief set in. Then followed anger, sadness, and shock. I didn't have much time to process, though. After a few weeks, Mike came and found me in Amarillo. He fell apart, rattling off a long list of excuses and promises:

It's just a phase. I'll get therapy. I'll go to AA. It's just a fantasy thing. It won't happen again.

All in all, I didn't want to get a divorce. We had made vows in front of God, and I didn't take that lightly. And obviously I didn't want to disappoint my family. I mean, I left Kylie for this man. It had to be for something.

So I went back to him.

They say that the best apology is changing your actions. If that's true, I got no real apology from Mike. After he brought me back to New Mexico, if anything, he got worse. His light drinking turned into nightly binges. Our disagreements escalated into screaming fights.

One night, I was vacuuming, and he had drunk a whole bottle of wine. He wanted me to drink with him, but half a glass will make my head spin. He didn't appreciate my no. He started yelling and threatening me. It went on for hours.

I was sitting on the blue chaise-lounge and finally stood up and started yelling back. The next thing I knew, I felt being slapped across my face. My thick square glasses went flying. I fought to stand—he slapped me again. The room was spinning, but I did hear him growl in pain. My little dog, a Westie, Fendi, had bitten him in the hand, but he kept grabbing at me. All I could do was scratch his bare chest to get him off.

I tried reaching for my phone, but Mike got there first. He hurled it across the room. It shattered into the wall, leaving a sizable hole. I tried to get out the front door but he just shoved me into it.

All I could do was think to myself, "I'm one of those people you see on TV." Never in a million years did I ever imagine abuse would happen in my home.

By the grace of God, he calmed down and finally fell asleep. I collapsed in the next room, checking my injuries and thanking God he hadn't hit me in the chest. (My sternum has already been broken four times.) Just the fear during that night I think was worse than the fight. I couldn't sleep, so afraid that he might wake up and hit me again.

That next morning, I called Kylie and Dad again. It was hard telling them what Mike had done to me. I wanted to be in control of my life, my marriage, and my own safety. Kylie, being the loving sister, was the first one to assure me that I had support. I remember her saying "You should have stabbed him!" It was dark, but it made me laugh. There was her spunk.

"Don't you get us in trouble again," I said.

Well, Dad and Kylie made another four-hour drive and helped me pack. They were getting to be pros by now.

I so wish I could say that was the last time. I wish that Mike hadn't come back to Amarillo and asked me one more time to come back. And I wish that I could say I sent him off with a boot to the pants.

But separation didn't come easily for me. If there was even a sliver of a chance that we could reconcile, my heart yearned for that.

Mike told me that we just needed to move again. "We'll get away from all this." And I wanted to believe that we could.

So we moved to Portland, Oregon. He had friends there and could still work. But the funny thing about being human is that we always take ourselves with us. We can run halfway around the world, but our shadow is always one step behind us. Mike and I didn't really need a new environment. We needed an inner miracle.

It took another year for the pain to finally push me to the final breaking point. Mike continued to cheat on me. He continued to drink. I locked myself in the bathroom one night. He busted down the door. He got drunk and locked me out in the icy Portland winter.

To keep the peace, I tried to ignore it. I tried to be the best wife, the kind of wife a man didn't "need" to cheat on.

But that was a false hope. Something had twisted in Mike's heart. I couldn't fix it for him. I couldn't fix it for me. One night I laid in our bed crying my eyes red, while he played Xbox in the other room. I could hear him talking to people through the headsets. He never sounded that energetic with me anymore.

I prayed, please give me a way out, God. Give me a way to escape.

The next morning I opened my eyes—they were still puffy from all the crying—and saw the light coming in softly from the corners of our blinds. There was light outside. No matter how dark it got in here, the sun shone on all the world out there.

I needed to get out there. I needed light. I needed hope.

That day, I packed up my clothes all by myself. All I had was my winter clothes because everything else was in storage. Softly whistling to my two dogs, I put everything in my black Mustang, looked back one last time—and hit the gas.

CHAPTER SEVEN

A Shy Return, A Warm Welcome

I ACCELERATED OUT OF THE NEIGHBORHOOD purely on muscle memory. My mind spun out of control. *Did I forget something? Is he coming after me? Is this the right way?* What did it matter anyway? If I got lost on the road, I wouldn't be any more lost than I felt inside.

Over the past four years I'd tried to align my life with someone who had claimed to follow the Lord but whose life didn't reflect it. And the harder I tried to make Mike happy, the farther I felt from true joy.

With Portland in the rearview mirror, I wouldn't get to Amarillo for three more days. I stopped at a gas station, halfway through Idaho. It was the first time I'd gotten out of the car since leaving. Pop the tank. Spin the cap. Swipe my card. Wrong way, flip it over.

Only one other pump had a car. The driver and I made eye contact for just a second. He nodded and looked back down at his phone. How could he not feel the hot distress radiating from my face? A satellite could probably see it from space.

After a few hundred miles, the anxiety softened. You can only ask the same questions so many times before your brain taps out. It felt like I was slowly wandering out of the wilderness. My eyes needed time to adjust to the new light.

At first, it felt like I'd lost the things around me. My husband. My house. My friends. But I'd lost more than that—before he and I even met. I thought clearing out of my crippling marriage might clear out my heart. But loss is like moving an old dresser back from the wall. Suddenly you find all the dirt, scraped paint, and dead bugs that never got cleaned. *Was it really here this whole time?*

No one tells you how to deal with twenty-nine years of emotional dust bunnies. I knew one thing for sure: *I can't do this alone.*

Throughout my adolescence and into my crazy twenties, faith had faded into the background. I knew God was there. I knew He took care of me, in a general way. But every day I'd woken up, put on my "big girl pants" and tried to take the steering wheel of my own life.

See what I can do, God?

In my desperate attempts to prove myself to everyone, it felt second-nature to try and prove myself to God. If I didn't measure up, well, then it was probably someone else's fault. It had to be. It couldn't be me. *I'm trying so hard.* Why would God love someone who had royally failed him—even after trying so, so hard?

The thought was crushing. So I didn't think about it as I pulled into Kylie's driveway. First thing through the door, I ran straight into her hug. My nephew, Keegan wrapped his own little arms around our legs.

Even though every "escape" before had ended with a return, this homecoming had a solid, more final feeling. Nuzzling into her shoulder, I said, "This is it. I'm not going back."

"You sure as hell aren't."

I smiled a little. "I mean, I *won't* go back. I...I feel—"

As tears caught in my throat, She held on a little tighter. "You're going to be okay, Yodi."

DRAWN BACK TO GOD

When Kylie and I were about seventeen years old, I called her "Yoda" out of the blue one day in our driveway. We fell apart laughing—I have no idea why or where it came from. Kylie and I had never even seen *Star Wars*! It's just not our kind of movie. (I'm more of a Hallmark kind of girl.) I called her Yoda and she called me "Yodi" along with some other endearing nicknames that I probably shouldn't share! She was so wise that Yoda fit her perfectly. Anyone that knows me, knows she was my Yoda.

There wasn't much to get out of the car. I had my winter clothes and two dogs. That was it. Kylie gave me $700 to get into an apartment of my own. It was just a bedroom, bathroom, and living/kitchen area. Small for sure, but the years had taught me that big and fancy didn't equal happiness.

Small and safe fit my bill. Well, my 150-pound Saint Bernard, Gracie, didn't appreciate it so much, but rebuilding takes time—whether it's a housing fund or confidence. Both had taken a real sucker punch.

Still, God had seen fit to bring me, safely, through those four years of crazy. There must be a reason. So I committed to a slow and steady rebuilding of my life. Whatever it took.

I'd gone out and given my own way a shot. A long shot. A four-year, knock-down, drag-out shot in the dark that left me on the ground more than once and eventually on the road back to Texas. (True Texans always find a way back!) But, more than that, I was on a road back to my faith.

I hadn't been to a church regularly since I was eleven years old. Those were the days we would pile into the red minivan and head into town. As a family, we would get out, Mom would smooth our matching dresses, fix our mussed hair, and walk us across the gravel parking lot—that ensured everyone wore sensible, God-fearing footwear. Hand in hand with Mom, Kylie and I felt right at home. She knew everyone, everyone knew her, and by proxy, everyone knew us before we could talk.

Kylie and I had our first spiritual awakening there. We buried our mother there. Church had been a gathering place, a landmark, and a reminder of life after pain.

In comparison, other churches felt like awkward, alien planets.

It had been emotional stress from dealing with Mike that first sent me back. He never wanted to go to church, but something tugged at my heart so strongly I couldn't ignore it. I found some comfort in those Sundays, away from Mike. But they also reminded me of the chasm between us, and the empty space in my heart. *Will I ever sit in a pew next to someone I love?* I missed walking the gravel path with Mom and Kylie. I missed sensing God's love in their very faces.

Back in Amarillo, I had the same feeling. I had family now; I had a safe home and a job—thanks to Kylie's reference—but there was a hole in my heart all the same.

Once again, I found myself in a church parking lot. I stayed in the car for a few extra minutes, just casing the place. *Which door is the best one? I don't want to look like a newbie. Ok, there are the front doors, but what if they opened straight into the sanctuary?!*

I got out and scanned the lot to see if anyone else had arrived late, too. Did I want to slip in on their coat-tails or beat them in? *Either way, in a church this size, they'll know I'm new.*

With a strength that could have only come from on high, my legs took me inside. The back pew was open. I slid in right as the congregation started singing:

On a hill far away stood an old rugged cross,

The emblem of suffering and shame,

And I love that old cross where the dearest and best,

For a world of lost sinners was slain....

For the next hour I sang and listened and cried. This wasn't a re-introduction between me and God. He knew me the whole time. Just like the Father knew his Prodigal Son the whole time he had wandered from home. He knew everything I'd done. The angry thoughts. The selfish actions. The "little" lies and justifications. He saw me drown high school sorrows in Smirnoff Ice. He saw me follow after a man who didn't honor Him. But in the end, God wanted me *home*. Not in Texas, but at the foot of the cross.

QUESTIONING GOD

In all honesty, I have asked God why He let certain things happen to me. Why did I feel such deep pain and betrayal? I haven't gotten answers for all my questions. But here's something: would it have been kinder for a loving Father to numb my pain without getting at the cause?

God loved me *too* much to let me stay comfortable with *less* than what He had planned for me. He could have eased my life just enough so that I thought I had it under control. I could have carried on doing my own thing, driving my life farther and farther from His will.

If I hadn't felt the tension, I might have stayed with a man who disrespected and disregarded me and our marriage. God had watched over my life, waiting for just the right time. This time, coming home meant not just a physical move, but a spiritual one.

As my spiritual life began to heal, so did my relationship with Kylie. Even though I'd left so quickly and been away so long, she welcomed me back in every way.

Now, she was committed to growing her family again—with a little girl.

Since having Keegan, she had been pregnant several times. Each one ended in miscarriage.

I opened her bathroom cabinet one day, and gasped. No exaggeration: over 100 pregnancy test sticks fell out! The clock was ticking on her heart valve, because it was only supposed to last for ten years, but she wasn't ready to switch it. It devastated us all watching her try so hard, but, of course, Kylie's grief was the worst.

Her heart condition made it tricky to find doctors to work with them. She and Derrick investigated IVF in Amarillo, but the pig valve was a liability. No one in Amarillo would touch it.

Did that stop my spunky sister? Absolutely not.

She found a specialist in Lubbock who agreed to help. We all found out pretty quickly why so many people had refused to do it. Because of her heart, Kylie needed blood thinners. But the IVF rounds required her to self-administer shots in her stomach.

One day, she asked me to do it for her, because it was too painful. I lifted her shirt and saw her whole stomach was black! I almost threw up giving her the shots. I felt like I was hurting Kylie more and that was the last thing I wanted to do.

Anything Kylie barely grazed would bruise her. Her energy was so low, but somehow she kept working sixty-hour weeks at the television station.

No one said what we were all thinking: *what if this doesn't even work?*

Every day I begged God to let the treatments work—but most of all to protect my sister.

BUTTERFLIES AND—A BROTHER?

In the meantime, our family was growing in other ways. Kylie and I had known all of our lives that we had been adopted. The details of our biological family were sketchy, known by some people, but always left up to us girls to figure out for ourselves.

At some point a family member had mentioned that our biological mother lived close by in Silverton, not even twenty minutes down the road from our childhood home. Her name, we were told, was Sabrina.

Kylie and I each processed the knowledge in different ways. Life had taken us around so many bends, that reconnecting with Sabrina had never made it to the top of our priorities. Our curiosity had stopped years ago. Neither of us imagined discovering other long-lost relations.

I was sitting on my couch one night in January of 2014 and got another Facebook message from my cousin. We weren't really close at the time, so it seemed a little strange. Her message just read, "I have to tell you something, but I don't want you to be upset."

What in the world? My gut reaction was that something bad had happened.

"You can tell me, I won't be upset."

She got right to the point: "You have a brother and he's been looking for you and Kylie."

What?

Our entire lives, Kylie and I had felt like the last two unicorns or something. Our temporary step-brothers had never felt like true siblings and, other than Dad, I didn't share family ties with anyone but my sister.

The story was shockingly simple. My cousin's best friend was married to a man named Matthew. Matthew had always known that he had older sisters that were given up for adoption. Twin sisters.

Well, when my cousin heard that, she started putting two and two together. What was Matthew's mom's name? Sabrina.

I couldn't believe there was someone else out there besides me and Kylie.

My cousin asked if we wanted to meet him. It was a lot to take in. Kylie wanted more time, and said no at first. I, on the other hand, needed to see my brother as soon as possible. The only conditions were that Matthew's wife would join us, and my cousin would come with me. We got dinner reservations at Chili's a week later.

My heart was full of so many butterflies. Here we were, two grown people, who could have grown up together, but were just now seeing each other for the first time.

I looked across the restaurant as we walked in. Anyone look like me? My cousin waved at one of the tables. The man stood up and waved back. He stood nearly six feet tall—you could tell by his build that he was a hard-working farmer—and his skin was a light chocolate color. I got closer and suddenly both of us couldn't stop grinning. We had the same smile!

I just couldn't believe it. Matthew was two years younger than me, almost to the day. He had lived with Sabrina for a little while, but had been mainly raised by his grandparents.

We swapped baby pictures and childhood stories. He had heard talk of his two lost sisters, but had no idea that we had been born with major heart problems.

The most shocking part of the night, however, was learning how many people knew about Matthew, my wonderful, kind, hardworking *brother* and never told me. This whole time, Matthew had grown up about fifteen minutes away from Silverton. We had been so close for our entire lives.

It did make me and Kylie upset to learn that most of our mom's family knew about Matthew and never told us. We were thirty years old when we found our brother, but he could have been there with us during all those hard times.

But had it not been for my cousin's message, I would never have known.

When I introduced our brother to Kylie—how many siblings get the opportunity to do that—she loved him just as quickly as I did. In the middle of our rebuilding, Kylie's fertility struggle, and other family stress, God had sent us the sweetest gift.

NEW LIFE, NEW HOPE

A few months later, on my way back from work, my purse started buzzing. It was a phone call from "Yoda." She was pregnant! By the grace of God I didn't run off the road in excitement.

But as exciting as the news was, everyone knew that Kylie's growing baby wouldn't be out of the woods for a while—and neither would Kylie.

During one of the most terrifying nights of her pregnancy, Derrick called me and the first words out of his mouth were, "Kylie's okay, but we are at the ER."

I hit my flashers and sped to the hospital. Kylie had suffered a seizure in her home. She had collapsed out of nowhere—Derrick and his brother caught her right before she hit the stone fireplace. Kylie had never had seizures before, but they became common during that pregnancy. I only saw one in person.

A harmless moment of laughter sent her head back, and the next thing we knew she started shaking. After that, anytime she laughed too hard, she went into seizures. The doctor gave her seizure medicines, but to everyone's frustration, she didn't take it. She refused to do or take anything that might harm the baby she was carrying. And she succeeded.

Carried to full term, Kenzie Jeanette Collins was born a day after Thanksgiving in 2015. It was a miracle. Blond hair, blue eyed, Kenzie looked like a princess in Kylie's arms. Of course we all bawled our eyes out. Of course her name had to start with a *K* just like ours, but her middle name was our mother Marsha's.

That same year, I met Brian. Well, I got set up on a blind date—by Kylie of course. The last time I got set up, however, was with Mike in Hawaii. *No thank you.* But Kylie was persistent.

"It'll be fun, no pressure, no worries. He's a nice guy." I rolled my eyes so hard. "No, really. Like a *good* guy. She really wanted me to have someone. And I appreciated that. So, for the heck of it, I went along.

Unbeknownst to me, Kylie had been trying to convince Brian to ask me out on a date for weeks. "You need to go out with my sister," she would repeatedly tell him. Brian was not only her former coworker, but truly one of her best friends. She had known him for several years, and they could and did talk about everything. He wasn't just a kind soul, he was also a twin, two minutes younger than his brother.

Knowing Kylie, I figured she had already told him anything and everything about me, so I really wasn't worried about talking about my heart problems or anything else for that matter when he picked me up on our first date.

He picked me up at my tiny apartment in his bright green polo shirt that matched his eyes perfectly. We went bowling and had the best time ever. They had a little bar inside the bowling alley so when we were done playing, we went in there to have a drink.

I must have either been too nervous, or had one sip too many because I spilled a beer over in his lap. He did nothing but laugh and wipe it up. He took me home after that and we watched Top Gun before I fell asleep on the couch.

He walked me to my bed and stayed with me so I wasn't alone. He was a complete gentleman the whole night, leaving me with a gentle kiss when he left. What I learned from that is anytime your sister wants to set you up with one of her best friends, let her!

It's a cliche, but God really does surprise you with the most beautiful things when you're not looking. Brian put me at ease in a way no other man had. Suddenly, I was spending time with a man who was nothing like my ex-husband. The difference was like day and night.

In moments where I expected anger, because that's where Mike would have been angry, Brian showed understanding. In moments where I expected lies or jealousy, Brian gave me honesty. My heart had a lot of healing still to do, but now, someone was walking beside me as I healed.

At my lowest moments, God sent me the comforting I never thought I deserved. He sent the comforting arms of my family—old and new—and of a loving man. My hope had begun to grow. I would soon need it more than ever.

CHAPTER EIGHT

"We're Your Daughters"

W HAT TRULY MAKES A FAMILY? I've had to tackle this question more than once over the past several decades. You can imagine families like you see in black and white TV times or childhood storybooks. But real life connections are messier. The longer you live and lose, the blurrier the lines get.

The average American family size is 3.14. That usually means two parents and one or two kids. For most of my life, I assumed that's what a family looked like. You may not stay together all the time. But you know that for better or for worse, that's your family. Biology never was all that important to me—except when it made me sick.

It didn't make a lot of sense to me, learning in science class that mothers and their biological children shared swirling hormones and pheromones of closeness and protection. That must not have happened with my mom. How could she have given us away otherwise?

I'd grown up with only one person who shared my DNA—Kylie. My biological mother had never shared a home or even a conversation with me. Somehow she was technically family—and not family at the same time. But our mother, Marsha, had taught us that family extends farther than blood relations. They say you can't choose your family. But Mom and Dad really did pick Kylie and me.

Growing up, my family were the people who cared for me on purpose. They were people who saw me grow up and knew my favorite things. Family makes things for you with their own hands, pushes you in wagons, and holds you in their arms. Family wakes up down the hall from you and comes in to tell you good morning.

If family is related to place and closeness, I certainly felt a connection to the people I grew up next to: Mom, Dad, Kylie, Kurby, and everyone else in our small town. But I'd also lived near people who had broken that family trust. I'd lived in houses where love was nowhere to be found. You can share a place with someone, but still never feel deep down in your heart that you're family.

Kenzie's birth marked over ten years since Kylie's heart surgery. The pig valve wasn't built to last much longer. It was finally time for her valve replacement surgery. But my sister wasn't ready to give anything up. She had a brand new baby. She was running a local television station, taking care of her dream home, a husband and two kids.

The replacement surgery would put her out of commission for half a year. She wouldn't be able to pick up her kids or go to work. And the first surgery had been traumatic. I know she was scared. And our lives were taking another turn for the complicated.

MORE SECRET DISCOVERIES

In the summer of 2018, our brother Matthew invited us over for dinner. We took turns going back and forth between towns for little reunions. Kylie and I loved every chance to spend time with Matthew. We just clicked. Pretty soon, walking into his house felt just as safe and inviting as walking into our own.

That night we'd gotten back on the subject of family. Curled up on the couch, I balanced a plate of chicken on my lap and said, "It's still amazing to me that we grew up so close. I wonder if we ever passed each other on the highway or something and never knew."

Matthew chuckled from his armchair. "It's something."

"Really," Kylie added, "Such a small world." She paused and continued, "It does make you think...."

"About what?" asked Matthew. I perked up, too.

"I mean, with us, in particular. Karlie and I thought we were the only ones, but of course with another Mom out there, why wouldn't we have a secret brother?"

She had a point. It had been thirty years and we hadn't spent much time thinking about our biological family.

"So," she continued, "we have a secret brother from a secret mom. What about a secret dad?"

Matthew breathed in through his teeth. "Careful what you wish for. Love her, but Momma didn't have good judgement." He got up, letting the armchair swing back. "And I don't know about meeting any more brothers—not after how Mark turned out."

Woah, woah, woah. Kylie and I shared a wide-eyed look. "*Mark?*"

No sound from Matthew in the kitchen. Kylie shouted, "Matthew, who is Mark?!"

He came back around the corner sheepishly. "Aw, I shouldn't have done that."

I squealed, "Another brother?"

Matthew danced around the topic for a few minutes, but when the Green twins gang up on you, it's easier to just surrender.

It turned out we did have a second "secret" sibling. Sabrina had gotten pregnant again a few years after Matthew was born. She had another boy and gave another gospel name, Mark. But neither boy could stay, not with her lifestyle. So, Sabrina's parents offered to raise them.

Matthew never forgot the tantrums Mark would throw. Matthew could still hear the angry words and curses he hurled at their grandparents. "We had the same situation, but something hurt extra bad with Mark. Something snapped."

Matthew told us how things got so bad with Mark's childhood behavior that at seven years old, his own grandparents sent him into foster care.

After that, we couldn't get any more information out of Matthew. He told us that Mark was "bad news" and we should leave it be. Just enjoy the good family we'd already found.

It made sense to leave things alone—things were crazy enough in our family. And we did trust Matthew's judgement. But it was just too hard to ignore a family revelation like that.

So Kylie and I went into full research mode. Every spare minute—at home, at work, everywhere—we searched and Googled and read anything we could find. Including the indictments.

Mark had several mugshots online for things from traffic tickets to felonies such as assault. He had done six years in prison and was up for parole when we found him. Even with that rap sheet, Mark was our brother. Our hearts did go out to him. We knew he had never had a real family, and that tugged at our heart strings. Visiting his prison would be a pretty big step, especially since he wouldn't know we were coming. I decided to write him a letter. I didn't say outright who I was, but asked him some questions, including what he might know about a couple of missing sisters.

MEETING OUR MOTHER

In the meantime, Kylie was making plans of her own. It was on a Sunday about a month after Mark's discovery. Kylie and I were supposed to go grocery shopping like we did together every Sunday. I hopped into Kylie's car, expecting the usual. Nope.

Kylie couldn't contain her emotion, "I found Sabrina, and we are *going*!" If I could have slammed on the brakes, I would have.

"Do what?!"

Kylie kept her eyes on the road, but smacked the top of the steering wheel for emphasis. "It's time. We're gonna do it."

"Hold on, you have her address?"

"Yup. She lives in Happy. Twenty minute drive. Easy."

I know better than to stop Kylie when she's on a roll, but I hadn't gotten any time to prepare. Neither had she. Credit where credit was due, though. All these years, I'd never been able to find anything public on our biological mother. We only knew she lived in the area through town gossip. We had never spoken, or even seen each other face to face.

"What are you gonna say?" Kylie always got fired up talking about Sabrina, but now all of those made-up arguments might actually happen.

"I don't know. I'm just gonna speak from the heart."

"Geez, okay. Just don't hit her."

We pulled up to a house that looked lucky to still be standing. Overgrown bushes covered old holes in the foundation. From where I stood, I could see rust spots on the tin roof. *Dear Lord,* I prayed in my head, *who are we going to find here?*

Kylie had a lot of anger and sadness towards Sabrina. It was this woman's fault her twin sister had been born with heart defects. She had sent us away. She had never cared to reach out. She had become a character in our minds—but in seconds we would meet the real person.

A few moments after we knocked, Sabrina opened the door. It was like Kylie had looked in a mirror. Except her reflection was more my size and had more wrinkles. She seemed to know exactly who we were at that moment.

For all the sass in the car, Kylie couldn't speak. Neither did Sabrina. They were two deer in each other's headlights. We all stood in complete silence.

All I could do was stick out my right hand and say, "Hi, Sabrina. My name is Karlie and we are the twins you gave away in 1984." She took a step back and put both hands to her face. Then she swung them wide and sprung forward for a hug.

"Oh my gosh, you're my girls." Her long, grey-black hair covered my face as she hugged me. I could smell alcohol. I could tell she'd had a rough life. Her house was falling apart on the inside as well as out. There were bottles and things covering the floors—and a hole in her bathroom floor that she told me not to fall into.

Suddenly, I thought back to the mother-child connection. What if Sabrina *had* kept us? I imagined her as a sixteen year old. Confused. Scared. Addicted. Would we have lived in a house like this all our lives? Would we have gone to Matthew's grandparents, too? Or would I have even survived? Probably not.

I imagined Kylie's spunk. Her sometimes sharp words and fierce nature—that she used for good to take care of me and others. What if it had snapped like this other brother we'd heard about? Would she have gone to foster care all alone?

A wave of thankfulness washed over me in that room. Teenage Sabrina didn't reject us. She saved us.

For the rest of our visit, Sabrina was kind and calm and answered all of our questions. I can't say if her answers were the complete truth, but it was a relief to have a response.

Kylie's rage had dwindled as well. Maybe she had similar thoughts as me, looking around the home, thinking about the future we might have shared. In all, we spent about twenty minutes in that living room together.

Sabrina asked us to come back and visit, and we said we would. There would be other opportunities to dig deeper into our biological mother's past.

As soon as we left Sabrina's, Kylie called Matthew.

"Well sis, did you meet ya' Momma?"

She laughed, "Ohh, you bet."

And I chimed in from the passenger seat, "She didn't even beat her up!" He was so happy that we had met her.

If we had grown up with Matthew—and somehow I'd survived childhood—I believe that we would have been okay. But things would have been very different. Family isn't just DNA and paternity tests. Bonds greater than blood connect us. And so I'm eternally thankful for the family Sabrina gave us when she gave us away.

FAMILY FRICTION

I got a letter back from Robertson prison in Abilene, Texes. It was from Mark. He'd responded quickly. I tore open the letter and started reading. The short version was that he hadn't heard of me, but still was kind.

I wrote to him again, this time mailing a picture of Kylie, Matthew, and me together. Hopefully, he would recognize his brother and put the pieces together. I explained to him our health issues and our childhood story.

Mark responded with shock. He said he was absolutely floored. He said his grandma had told him he had twin sisters out there, but he never believed her. His replies always sounded genuine, like he truly cared. He said he didn't know what our diseases were but was going to start researching it right away.

Mark got transferred to a place for pre-release parolees in the fall of 2018 and was scheduled for full release in March of 2019.

Every other family "reunion" had gone well so far, so Kylie and I decided to visit him in prison.

The facility was much less intense than the ones I saw on TV shows. We still had to go through a metal detector, but I carry a special card with me for places like the airport and stuff because I can't go through them with my pacemaker.

"It's a pacemaker," I told the guard in the navy coat. He might have guessed already from our matching red outfits I'd made for a Heart Walk. Kylie's shirt said *I Survived Heart Surgery*. Mine said *I Survived Heart Surgery x 4*.

There weren't any decorations hung in the visiting room, just some filing cabinets and a beige clock tick, tick, ticking on the wall. Mark was sitting at a small metal table in the middle of the visiting room. When he saw us, he immediately stood up. He shared his brother's dark skin and tall stature. I couldn't help but remember the way Matthew had jumped up in that Chili's. After hugs and introductions, we all started crying.

The guard made a comment, "Hey, y'all look alike. Any relation?" It made us laugh. Physically, none of us looked like we should be related. But it was all in the smiles. I made it a point to say, "Yes, but I'm the oldest of us all." We stayed for the entire 4-hour time slot. The visit was so sweet that we all cried *again* when it was time to go.

We visited once a month for the next several months. In the beautiful pink haze of this newly discovered family, everything seemed just perfect. Anything Mark said, we assumed the best of him. He had had such a sad life, and now we wanted to see him succeed. Maybe our family's love would rub off and create new, happy memories.

Mark was allowed phone calls if we put money on his phone. Of course we wanted to talk, so we sent some whenever he needed it. But then, the calls increased. And soon it started to be only Kylie's phone that rang more often.

It got to a point where every time Kylie would come over to my house, she was on the phone with Mark. One time, she didn't answer the first time he called. It kept ringing. And ringing. She finally picked up, and I heard an angry voice on the other end, "*Why didn't you pick up the phone?*" I made a face at Kylie. But she didn't look me in the eye.

It was my first clue that things weren't all they seemed to be with Mark.

We all believed in the power of change. I mean, just look at our lives. Both Kylie and I had made some bad decisions in the past. But we didn't define ourselves by those mistakes and sins.

God had chosen to bring restoration and redemption into my life, after a hard childhood, after hard physical problems, after a horrific marriage and divorce. Am I the same person who went through that? Don't people change?

It didn't even cross my mind that a brother would manipulate his own family, because I believe that is what he did. I blame myself in a lot of ways for bringing him back into our lives. But who could have known? Well, maybe Matthew did. But we had pushed past his protests. Had I not written to him, had we not wanted to help him get his life on track, maybe what happened next might have been different?

CHAPTER NINE

Walking Alone

I F YOU WERE GRANTED THE opportunity to peek into the future, would you do it? I don't mean winning lottery tickets or horse races. I mean, would you want to know *your* future?

At first glance, knowing what will happen to us may seem exciting. So many of our worries come from trying to guess the future, plan the future, or control the future—but no matter what, the future never fully cooperates. Maybe knowing exactly what's going to happen would help us prepare better for disasters or changes. Then again, if we knew what would happen, the good, the bad, and everything else, how might that affect our present?

Instead of worrying about what *could* happen, we would probably spend every minute *still* worried about what was coming. No matter how many good things have happened, the certainty of loss can snatch control of the steering wheel of our peace.

I'd always been certain that my family would lose me one day. My heart condition should have killed me long ago. I don't know of anyone else with the same one who has lived so long that has had as many surgeries and a pacemaker installed like I have.

My sister watched me survive four open-heart surgeries. Any of them could have ended my life. And after each surgery, our moments together felt more precious. Life is a blessing for sure, but one we've known could change at any moment.

By 2019, Kylie and I had come a long way since cruising together in the red wagon. We'd both learned a lot of independence and endured some of the most painful days of our lives without each other. Instead of one girl pulling the other, we had started walking side by side. Sometimes we walked apart, but coming back together always felt right.

Kylie and I each had a rock to return to as sisters who know everything and love unconditionally.

On July 8th 2019, I walked out of my front door and went two houses down to Kylie's. (Yep, we were finally neighbors.)

In front of her house was a new maroon Ford Explorer. It was a perfect match to mine in every way except color. Mine is silver. I looked around to see if anyone else was in the house. Our half-brother Mark had gotten out on parole recently and had instantly made himself a fixture in Kylie's home. At first we were glad to have him out. Everyone deserves a second chance at freedom, right?

But that was the problem. He didn't seem interested in getting out there and doing life stuff. He just stayed very near Kylie.

She thought I was just jealous. After all, we'd never really had to share siblings with anyone else. But I thought back to our relationship with Matthew. There'd been no jealousy there, just joy. He always had the feeling of safety, peace, boundary, and encouragement.

Mark gave me altogether different vibes. Try as I might, every time he and I were in the same room, my red flags flew sky high. I noticed it in small things first—how he always asked for things, how it upset him to wait, how he got mad at the littlest inconvenience, and how Kylie took the brunt of it all. Then he escalated.

Kylie got him a job—that he immediately quit. Kylie got him into college classes—that he quickly dropped. I wondered at first, did he just want independence? Unlikely. Mark pretty much lived at Kylie's house. He ate her food, used her car, and spent her credit cards.

That made me see *red*. And it concerned me that Kylie didn't. This person was taking advantage of her, but she didn't care. Did she want someone to protect again, like she'd always had me to protect?

So that day, with Mark out of the house, I breathed a little easier. Kylie had called me and asked if I had any cough medicine because she was very sick. When I said sure, that she could walk over and get it, she told me, reluctantly, that she didn't have the strength to walk. *Strange*, I thought. In the spring of that year, she'd had a heart echo done. Her cardiologist had checked everything. I knew because Kylie had forwarded me the doctor's voicemail. The nurse's voice sounded chipper and excited. Kylie's heart looked great.

"You were saying?" Kylie had replied, definitely smug. I had been on her butt for years to get her aortic valve replaced, but I was willing to be wrong a million times over if it meant that my sister was healthy. I just couldn't get the thought out of my mind. *Ten years. The valve is made to last ten years.*

"MORE THAN ANYTHING, YODA"

I walked into her house to find Kylie on the couch with several blankets and a humidifier going right beside her. Her skin was so pale, her breathing slow and delicate. I'd only seen her that sick once before. I knelt down to hold her hand, and we both started crying.

I told Kylie I was going to call my boss at the hospital. Maybe they could get her in the next day. I'd have to walk back to my house to get my cell phone.

"I will call you in ten minutes, okay? Ten minutes." *Ten. Ten. Ten.* She nodded and closed her eyes. Before I left her house, I said, "Don't move. Don't get up. *Don't do anything.*"

She replied, "Yes, I'll be good."

"Lay here and relax, and I'll call you."

I walked home and called my contact, but since my hospital connection wasn't in cardiology he couldn't help me get her in. He said, "Don't cry, Karlie. It's not like she's gonna die tomorrow."

I called my sister back to give the update—she had me on speaker phone.

"Are you... driving?" I asked.

"Maybe."

I heard a voice in the background. Male, mumbling, familiar. *Oh, hell no!*

"Kylie, go home! You might be dying. I can't even... what are you doing?"

"Mark was out of ice cream at home. We're just getting some real quick"

I couldn't believe it. Five minutes ago my sister couldn't get off the couch, but Mark needed *a snack?*

I couldn't keep the fury out of my voice, "Why the hell does he need ice cream? How selfish can—

"Karlie, how 'bout you mind your own *damn business!*" And she hung up.

I knew my sister's sickness wasn't a fluke. But there was nothing I could do.

Three days later, I got a call from my dad at work. Kylie was at the hospital in Amarillo. She hadn't called me. She hadn't texted. Furious and anxious at the same time, I called the hospital. Someone had assigned security questions to her name, so they couldn't give out her hospital room. It seems Mark had struck again, but he seriously underestimated the shared knowledge of twins. I knew every answer to any question Kylie could come up with, so I found her room pretty fast.

But I still arrived too late. As I pulled into Amarillo Hospital, Dad called again. "They're moving her to Lubbock for open heart surgery." Crap.

An hour's drive later, Dad and I burst into Kylie's hospital room. My fears were confirmed. Mark sat next to Kylie's bed. If they'd been talking, they got quiet quickly when we came in. Instead of a warm welcome, I got a dirty look from Mark.

Dad asked, "Can we have a minute to talk to her?" Mark looked indignant. He said that anything we needed to say he could listen to. Kylie didn't say anything. Mark straight-up refused to leave the room. I think he knew that if we got Kylie alone she might open up to us. She might realize he was bad news.

Kylie's husband eventually arrived and the drama settled down momentarily. I needed time to process what was going on. The woman in the hospital bed was Kylie, but not the Kylie I'd grown up with.

Kylie finally got back to a room and was hooked up to IV's, which she hated. She hated anything to do with doctors. If one tech missed a vein, or tried to tell her something she didn't like, Kylie cussed them straight out. But even her sass couldn't hide how sick she was.

Doctors requested more than once to put her in the cardiac ICU, but Kylie refused. It didn't make sense, but no one could reason with her. She yelled and cussed at everyone. Except Mark. I couldn't understand the hold he had on her.

On July 11, she was scheduled for her Aortic Valve replacement surgery. Finally. It had been nearly fifteen years since her first valve placement in 2004.

The day of the surgery, I pulled some strings to speak with Kylie alone. Through the dark circles and pieces of sweaty hair on her pale forehead, I needed to find my sister. I had to see *her* under all the anger and fear and silent treatment.

When she met my eyes, after moments of silence, I finally did.

I saw the inclusive toddler pushing me in my diaper box. The brave explorer leading me into playground adventures. I saw the best friend who always snuck into my room to snuggle. And the depressed teenager, beaten down, screamed at, and yet still persevering. This was the woman who answered my hysterical phone call after Mike's abuse. My yoda.

And while I could have stayed angry at how she—and Mark—had chosen to treat us, the overwhelming love for my sister was stronger.

We grabbed hands, just like little girls in Silverton. I could feel the stinging tears coming, so I tried to get the words out quickly. "I'm proud of you. I love you. I will always be here."

She kept the same expression, but tightened her hand. I continued, hearing footsteps in the hallway, "Mom would be so proud of the mother you are. I love you more than anything, Yoda. *Anything.*"

We'd had less than a minute alone when Mark stomped into the room. Gosh darn, I could have spit.

I kissed Kylie on the forehead and sat by her side until the doctors came to take her back.

Dad and about ten family members were in a different waiting room where families wait for the surgeons. This surgery will change Kylie's life for the better, I thought. With a new heart, we could get her back on her feet. Like she helped me rebuild my life, we were going to support her in building hers. I hoped and prayed it wouldn't include *both* half-brothers.

Our whole family sat together, across the room from Mark. He had a hand on all of her bags, like someone was going to steal them. We sat there for the next five hours.

Then two surgeons walked in. If it wasn't on a pacemaker, my heart might have beaten out of my chest. They asked immediate family members into a tiny office to give us the results.

The next event happened before I could blink.

As soon as we got up, Mark bolted. In each arm he scooped up Kylie's bags. Her car keys clinked with each of his strides. Dad gasped. Before anyone even knew if Kylie survived, our own brother had bolted with her possessions. We watched him go but had more important issues to deal with. The cardiothoracic surgeon, Dr. Paone was speaking in a quiet tone, "I'm very sorry. She has twenty-four hours."

Then I heard a scream.

It took a moment to realize that the person who started screaming was me. After everything she and I had lost together, I had never prepared to lose her. Not for good. Not like this.

It had always been *me* who was sick. It had always been *me* who was in the hospital. It was always *me* that was going to die first.

For the next half hour my breaths happened in wet gasps. I couldn't believe what I heard. Twenty four hours? Time didn't seem real anymore.

Hours later when she was stable enough, we got to go into the Cardiac ICU and see her. Kylie was unrecognizable. I had never seen anything like it. I just held her hand, swollen three times the normal size, and started praying. *God please, please wake her up.*

An ECMO machine (for short-term life support) was keeping her blood oxygenated. The new doctor said that there was no way in hell her heart was fine when she had gotten that all- clear voicemail previously. It seems her heart valve had been leaking for the last two to three years. Because Kylie's valve had been leaking blood onto her heart, it meant that it had worked overtime to move the blood off.

Kylie's heart damage was irreversible. I was going to lose my sister.

NEEDING A MIRACLE

It was July 28, 2019, and I didn't know what to do. All control had left me. For some reason, I felt like contacting an old family friend, Jim Browning.

Any time I think of a person close to God, I think of him. Jim had been our preacher in Silverton when I was around five or six years old. He and his wife Jan had also been my mom's best friends. Jim had left our tiny church and joined the military as a chaplain. I had seen him one time probably a decade before. The last trip we ever took with Mom was to San Antonio to see Jim and Jan. Every time I see him, I cry because I think of Mom.

I had no way of contacting Jim, but his daughters were both friends on Facebook. I messaged one of them just wondering if Jim could call me and pray with me. They had no idea what was going on with Kylie. Not even twenty minutes later, my phone rang. Unknown number. I answered. It was Jim!

I poured out my heart and soul to Jim, someone I hadn't seen or talked to in years. But he listened patiently. I told him how Kylie was overdue for heart surgery, how Mark had come into our lives as a hopeful new brother but had taken everything he could from Kylie.

Jim talked with me for a solid thirty minutes and then asked if he could pray with me.

"Please." I responded.

We had returned home to get some rest and we were headed back when the phone rang again. Dad was crying on the other end. I told Brian to pull over and let me drive because he didn't speed and we needed some speed. I didn't even get out of the car. He got out and went around while I hopped over the console. I put my flashers on and set the cruise at ninety-two mph. I passed two state troopers, but somehow God got me there safely without being stopped.

Kylie had been put back on the ECMO because she wasn't doing better. In fact, she was slowly getting worse. It was around lunchtime and Dad, Brian and I were the only ones at that time at the hospital. Dad had called the whole family and told them they needed to get back up to the hospital. No matter who went home to get some rest or to go somewhere to eat, Kylie was never alone. My aunt and uncle had practically moved in. They bought me new shoes, a blanket to keep me warm, plenty of food and never left our sides.

Then another miracle happened. We were sitting out in the hall outside the ICU when I looked up to see Jim Browning, in the flesh, walking my way. But he lived over seven hours away! *How is this happening?* It was perfect, God-sent timing that I'd messaged his daughter that day, because Jim happened to be visiting a relative's house— only an hour away. I had no clue.

I just hugged him and cried. It felt like God had sent me that hug personally.

All of our family started showing again after lunch. The doctors called Derrick, Dad, Jim, Brian, and me to a back room in the ICU. He hemmed and hawed for a minute, then broke the news. They had done everything they could. Her heart had been okay, then it went rapidly downhill. Her lungs weren't working on their own. Her kidneys had shut down. Her body had been through so much.

We went out to the waiting room. Dad walked out a few minutes later from the double doors that lead to patient rooms. He moved very solemnly, sat down and then said very calmly, "Kylie went into A-FIb. They had to shock her."

I've had A-FIb. I know what it does to a person's heart. Kylie was already so sick. I knew right then she wasn't going to make it.

"They had to shock her twice." I lost it again.

The doctors told us we all needed to go say our goodbyes.

I still can't believe the miracle that Jim was there. He helped every one of my family back to Kylie's room and just stayed with them while they said goodbye. He held on to me so tightly while he walked me back there. I told Kylie how much I loved her and begged her not to leave me. I told her she was my whole life. She couldn't respond. The last thing that Brian said to Kylie, one of his best friends, was, "I'll always take care of Karlie for you."

If God could have given me a glimpse of that day beforehand, I don't know if I could have lived my life. We can only truly handle grief as it comes. And, friends, it is heavy. If you've had to go through similar events, you know what I'm talking about.

Walking out the door to her hospital room was the hardest thing I've ever done. I think it was only with the hands of God on my shoulder that it happened at all. Kylie was out of my hands. Truly she never had been in my hands, not ultimately. But she had always been in His.

After everyone had said goodbye, the doctor came out with a tear in his eye and we knew. He handed Dad a small vial with a little piece of paper inside. It contained a single scratchy blip: Kylie's last heartbeat.

CHAPTER TEN

Reflections of Faith

MY SISTER KYLIE WAS JUST thirty-five that day—the same age as our mother when she passed. We were eleven. So was Kylie's son, Keegan. The feelings flooded back, like living two traumas simultaneously.

Again I shouldered the shock of outliving another irreplaceable woman. *That should have been me.* Brian put his arm around me and together we slowly made our way to the car.

But walking out of the hospital on my own two feet felt like a mistake. I'd prepared to say goodbye one day—from the surgery bed myself. In the commotion, our roles had gotten switched. *What movie were we living in now?* I didn't know my lines anymore.

We sat down in the car but didn't crank the key. Suddenly the grief surged. It was tangible pain, a squeezing, or maybe an expansion, like my heart would literally burst out of my chest. Brian held my hand as the sobs racked my body. I could barely breathe between the hyperventilating and the half-suppressed wails.

It's almost unfair the amount of grief a human can experience. I imagined that at certain levels a person would just pass out from the intensity. But not for me.

No deep grief is just one category of feeling. If you feel loss, you might feel anger too. You might feel shame or confusion. You may not accept the pain at all—or bargain it away in your head. You begin sifting through old memories, all of the things you'll miss, and then fall apart with the realization that you'll never live them again.

With each new wave of emotion, you acclimate a little more to the new normal. Your heart does its research: *First Monday without Kylie, and I'm still alive. First Tuesday without Kylie, and I'm still alive.*

Then you go to the grocery store for the first time without your sister. And it sucks. And you cry in every aisle. But you're still alive—and your heart records another kind of day that you can survive.

Anyone who has lost deeply has asked God the question: *Why? What is the reason for this?*

Sometimes the answer is revealed; sometimes it isn't. For me, talking to God about Kylie hurt for a while. In the hospital, I'd been on my hands and knees begging for Him to save her life. Many people have been there. Sometimes I try and wonder just how many prayers come out of hospital rooms—prayers that may have never been spoken before.

The Christian walk might look strange to an outsider. It's not automatically easier. Easy would be walking blindly through the dark. But then you can't even see what's there to hurt you.

It's not easy to know the truth and hold onto it in a world that will fight you tooth and nail to just let go. But walking through life without hope? That's nearly impossible. And the truth, that the world says is silly and old and uncool, really does set you free.

Because the truth is, it's not about how hard we can hold onto Christ. He is already holding us tightly. If we can live as people who are already held—instead of people who have no one to turn to—the burden of carrying the whole world lifts from our shoulders.

Living with that trust changes everything.

REFLECTIONS ON FAMILY

Every now and then, I've gotten to realize the timing of God's plan in the moment. But usually, for me, recognizing it takes time. Only looking back, can I see all the puzzle pieces fitting together.

Who knew that the scared teenager in Silverton, Texas, would be brought to the exact right people? Who knew she would cross paths with a couple with no kids, hospital experience, and the deep desire to create a family? When I think about how differently our lives might have been, in a tragic way, I can't help but thank God for his hand over us.

With every up and down my family has experienced, I truly wouldn't trade them for the world. Each argument and reconciliation has made me the woman I am and brought my faith through every right twist and turn. Kylie's and my adoption reminds me of the adoption we have in the Gospel. We were *all* born spiritual orphans, trying to take care of ourselves, scrambling for safety and acceptance—and failing miserably.

For no other reason than *love*, God picked us to be His children. He *wanted us* to be heirs of His eternal kingdom. We hadn't proved ourselves lovable, just like newborn Kylie and Karlie couldn't prove ourselves lovable. (In fact, we were extra sick and hard to keep.)

The sacrifice of my adopted mother and father reflects the sacrifice of Christ for the world, who *"for the joy set before him, endured the cross, despising the shame, and is set down at the right hand of the throne of God."* (Hebrews 12:2)

You don't choose your family, and you don't even choose who chooses you. Each person is unique, with a will of his or her own. A lack of control is built into human relationships. We want it, though. We want it badly. (I speak from experience.) And we can spend lifetimes trying to feel like we have a handle on the way people act. It's a great distraction from trying to handle our own actions.

When I watch the people I love do things that hurt themselves, it hurts. Sometimes it hurts physically. That pain is a sign that I want a different role—one that was never actually given to me. It's the role that Adam and Eve were offered in the garden: *to be sovereign like God.*

If only they would do things like I do.

If only they would stop doing that thing I hate.

If only they knew what was good for them.

Someone once said that sadness is the result when God stops doing my will. Ha! Isn't that the truth? But there's a reason *He* is Father and I am His child.

When things happen that I can't explain or understand, He gathers me up into loving arms and holds me in all the pain.

I am thankful for the Psalms in the Bible, some of which are shockingly sad and angry. The Psalmist comes to the Father with every emotion in his heart, knowing that God listens to them all. And the Father didn't turn the Psalmist away for his hard thoughts. Instead He guided him through the difficulty—and after every dark night, joy came in the morning.

REFLECTIONS ON ANGER

Speaking of hard feelings, I do wish that I could have taken more hard knocks for Kylie. I still process the frustration with men and women who did her wrong.

Part of me can't handle the anger I feel towards my half-brother Mark. His story is still playing out, still clashing with members of my family, still fighting for his piece of Kylie's life.

When I think about him, the blood boils in my head. My shoulders tense, and I just want to scream. My sister was in such a vulnerable place, and he took advantage of that. And now she's gone. He can't make it up to her. He can't bring her back. It feels like my body can barely hold all of the emotion.

But when I can step back, I also know that the real enemy is much bigger than people. Every hurt and every perversion in Mark's life happened as the result of a broken world and a broken spirit of sin.

Our conflict isn't ultimately with another human being but with evil in this world. Ephesians 6:12 says, "For we do not wrestle against flesh and blood, but against principalities, against powers, against the rulers of the darkness of this age, against spiritual *hosts* of wickedness in heavenly *places*."

Mine *and* Kylie's true fight was and is against the rulers of darkness. And in the end, whatever happens, that's Mark's fight too.

The fact that the darkness had been pulled back from *my* heart, that I had been given new life and new motivations and a new desire to love—that was a gift from God. I could have just as easily grown up like Mark. And that's humbling to realize. I grew up with the gift of my mother's faith. Mark didn't.

Of course, it's easier to say this than to really feel it. Righteous anger feels *good* in a way. And sin should never be excused or celebrated. But pure anger and punishment doesn't bring reconciliation. Every day I stay angry, it's another day that the enemy has a toehold in my heart.

Anger

But anger and fear can't stay forever. It can't be allowed to enslave me. It reminds me what the Apostle Paul wrote:

For you did not receive a spirit of slavery that returns you to fear, but you received the Spirit of sonship, by whom we cry, "Abba! Father!" The Spirit Himself testifies with our spirit that we are God's children. And if we are children, then we are heirs: heirs of God and co-heirs with Christ—if indeed we suffer with Him, so that we may also be glorified with Him. (Romans 8:15-18)

My pain is still fresh, but every day I have a choice—anger or love. Frustration or peace. Some days peace wins. Some days it doesn't. And that's all part of the Christian walk. Christ has felt our difficult feelings too. He felt sadness, loss, hunger, betrayal, separation, even apprehension at his own death.

But Romans 8 continues, with hope:

Romans 8

We know that the whole creation has been groaning together in the pains of childbirth until the present time. Not only that, but we ourselves, who have the firstfruits of the Spirit, groan inwardly as we wait eagerly for our adoption as sons, the redemption of our bodies. For in this hope we were saved; but hope that is seen is no hope at all. Who hopes for what he can already see? But if we hope for what we do not yet see, we wait for it patiently.

In the same way, the Spirit helps us in our weakness. For we do not know how we ought to pray, but the Spirit Himself intercedes for us with groans too deep for words. And He who searches our hearts knows the mind of the Spirit, because the Spirit intercedes for the saints according to the will of God....

For I am convinced that neither death nor life, neither angels nor principalities, neither the present nor the future, nor any powers, neither height nor depth, nor anything else in all creation, will be able to separate us from the love of God that is in Christ Jesus our Lord. (Romans 8:22-39)

The Son of God—fully God *and* fully human like us—went through the worst, so that we could know that whatever life throws at us, he has already conquered it. He understands and wants to give us freedom.

REFLECTIONS ON DEPENDENCE

We Texans are big on independence. We don't like being told what to do. *Don't Tread on Me* and all that good stuff. But the power of a life in Christ builds on something else. Self-will and "spiritual independence" won't get you too far—at least not far in the right direction. The Gospel requires dependence on someone greater and stronger and more reliable than a human being. And that's the *best news* we can hear.

For the rest of my life, I will depend on a pacemaker. It is attached to my heart, the organ that keeps me alive. The pacemaker makes sure that my heart doesn't go too fast…or too slow. Because either one would kill me.

Now, if I suddenly decided that I wanted to call the shots again—*ugh, 80 bpm is so constricting*—and tried to take it out, where would that get me? Freedom and health and a new life? No, my heart is naturally broken. I'd more likely end up with a hospital bill, if not a funeral bill.

My physical heart, on its own, is broken beyond my ability to heal it. My spiritual heart is also fatally diagnosed without the outside intervention of a Savior.

Remember David and Goliath? Everyone freaked out when a little shepherd boy decided to take on the Philistine giant. And, really, David should have been squashed. But when Goliath laughed in his face and challenged his God, David didn't rely on his skill or his strength. He said, "You come at me with a sword and a shield, but I come against you in the name of the LORD Almighty, the God of the armies of Israel, whom you have defied." (1 Samuel 17:45)

God used a little shepherd boy and some stones to overturn Israel's biggest enemy. It shouldn't have happened—and it wouldn't have, without God.

All of the growth I've experienced over these past decades can only have come from God. He has cared for me time and time again. He was with me through every day, even when I didn't feel near Him. It wasn't God that moved. He is the same from Texas to Hawaii to Oregon to wherever life takes you.

Without a trust in God, I don't know how I would have carried the loss of my mother, my marriage, my sister, and my own independence. I'm learning every day that while faith doesn't prevent tragedy, it will get you through it.

I can look to the future with hope. I can know that God has my mother and my sister in His arms. I can believe that nothing will stand between the love of God and me. And that changes everything.

Kylie, my precious sister and best friend, enjoy the presence of God until I see you again.

I'm saving the biggest hug for you.

REFLECTIONS ON ANSWERS

I wish that the lessons I've learned could tie up all of my struggles in a neat bow. It would be great if every difficulty ended with a simple moral lesson. But, like you, as long as I'm living, I'm learning. The past thirty-six years have given me amazing tools for growth, understanding, forgiveness, and perseverance. A loving God gives me these tools every single day. And I'm still learning how to use them best for his glory.

Along the way, I hope to share them with other people. And I hope to share my tried and tested belief that even through the struggle, God is with me and He is good. But I'm still learning.

I am still learning how to be alone. To this day I deal with deep feelings of loneliness without Kylie. I always had a lifeline with her to call, to visit, to help me with anything. Grief is a process. It comes back in waves. And God has given me friends and family to walk me through even the hardest days. He is still so good.

I wrestle at times with feelings of abandonment. My mother died, then my sister—who took care of me like a mother. I still ask God sometimes, "Why did you let this happen to me?"

But faithfulness does not require every answer. Romans 8:28 says that God is working all things for our good. I am learning that everything happens for a reason whether we agree with the outcome or not. He is still so, so good.

None of us can hold it together on our own. Sometimes we need that extra inspiration, the hope and the faith that things are going to get better. So I ask you:

➤ Where is your hope when darkness, sadness and tragedy begin to consume you? Do you look to God or to somewhere else?

➤ Were you born with something you still struggle with? Were you diagnosed and wonder how could God do this to me?

➤ Did something tragic happen and now you're tempted to be angry at God?

I've had to wrestle with all of these questions. When people ask me about why I might have been born with my heart condition, I think of a certain bible passage. In John 9, Jesus's disciples asked him about a man who had been born blind—*who sinned for him to be this way?* He answered them, no one's specific sin caused his blindness. Instead Jesus said that the man was perfectly positioned for the works of God to be revealed in Him. I pray that is the case with me. I long to have his work revealed through my story.

My physical limitations are not a punishment or a reason for guilt. Instead, the extent of my life struggle reveals the even greater extent of power and glory that my God has. That truth is exactly what I want to share with my life.

My circumstances and yours can be an opportunity to show what God can truly do.

It's because of His mercy and love that I have been able to persevere.

It's because of a Good Father that I am free to wrestle with hard questions.

It's because of a grace that I could never earn, that I know I will never be able to lose it—and I can live without fear or shame in the power of a new name—Child of God!

My broken heart is now one with His.

ABOUT THE AUTHOR

KARLIE GREEN IS AN AUTHOR, speaker, and friend to women facing struggles in life. Born with life-threatening heart defects, she entered the world five minutes before her twin sister Kylie. As a sister, daughter, friend, and survivor of four open heart surgeries and significant life challenges, she believes sharing stories is one of the most powerful ways to connect and heal. Karlie currently lives in Amarillo, Texas with her family, her community of friends, and her two dogs.

To contact Karlie directly, email her at
Karlie@KarlieGreen.com
or visit her website at *KarlieGreen.com*

ACKNOWLEDGEMENTS

THIS JOURNEY AND THE PEOPLE who have helped me along the way have been a gift from God. Without their help, prayers, and encouragement, I couldn't have made it this far.

First, to Bill Blankschaen and his amazing StoryBuilders team, thank you for all the countless hours and work y'all have put in to help make my dream of writing and publishing a book come true. This has been one of the most amazing experiences of my life. Y'all have helped me grow in ways I never thought possible. Akemi, you are not only an amazing project leader, but a dear friend. Thank you for talking to me at times when I needed it and helping me every step of the way.

To Annie. Thank you for your truth, your words, and your honesty. Since day one when I began this journey, you have believed in me when I didn't believe in myself. Your prayers are so deep and wonderful, the whole world would be as blessed as I am to hear them and learn from them.

To Kurby. My oldest and dearest friend. You are a true blessing from God. Although we were far apart for many years, it was like nothing had changed. You have been there for me when I have needed you most. No friend has ever supported me like you have. Thank you for your friendship and our wonderful memories.

To Aunt Dorothy. Everyone in the world should have an "Aunt Dorothy." That's why I didn't say *my* Aunt Dorothy. Ever since I got that news last July, you haven't left my side. You held me when I needed it most. You have been a sister to me, a mother to me, and one of my best friends. Everything I have needed, you have been. You are the kindest, most selfless person I know. You always know exactly the right thing to say no matter what the situation is. I thank God every day that mom left me with such an amazing aunt. Please never stop being you, and never stop baking goodies for me and Brian (especially your mini-cinnamon rolls).

To my Daddy. Thank you for always making sure I was ok. You have sacrificed a lot for me and Kylie over the years, and I am grateful.

Last, but certainly not least, to Brian. The love of my life and my best friend. When I told you that I wanted to write a book, you were so encouraging to me. You have always told me to follow my dreams and never give up. You make me want to be a better person. God blessed me so much when he brought you into my life. Thank you for loving me. And thank you for being you. I love you.

Made in United States
North Haven, CT
11 October 2021

10278080R00075